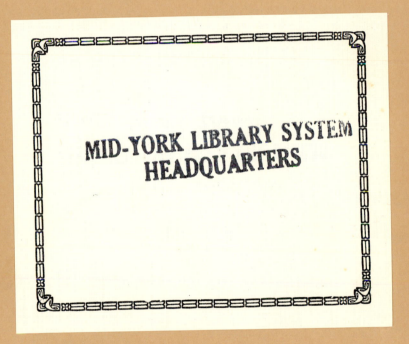

THE DICTIONARY OF
FOOD
AND WHAT'S IN IT
FOR YOU

THE DICTIONARY OF
FOOD
AND WHAT'S IN IT
FOR YOU

BARBARA LEVINE GELB

PADDINGTON
PRESS LTD
NEW YORK & LONDON

For my mother and my father

Library of Congress Cataloging in Publication Data

Gelb, Barbara Levine, 1931-
 The dictionary of food and what's in it for you.

 Includes index.
 1. Food—Composition—Tables. I. Title.
TX551.G28   641.1   77-20973
ISBN 0-448-22365-1

Filmset in England by Whitecross Graphics Ltd.,
177/187 Whitecross Street, London
Printed and bound in Scotland by
Morrison & Gibb Ltd., Edinburgh

Illustrations by Eileen Batterberry

IN THE UNITED STATES
PADDINGTON PRESS
Distributed by
GROSSET & DUNLAP

IN THE UNITED KINGDOM
PADDINGTON PRESS

IN CANADA
Distributed by
RANDOM HOUSE OF CANADA LTD.

IN SOUTHERN AFRICA
Distributed by
ERNEST STANTON (PUBLISHERS) (PTY) LTD.

CONTENTS

ACKNOWLEDGMENTS & SOURCES

The data in this book have been based mainly on the U.S. Department of Agriculture's *Composition of Foods* by B. Watt and A. L. Merrill (Agricultural Handbook no. 8, 1975) and its supplement, *Composition of Foods: Dairy and Egg Products* by the Consumer and Food Economic Institute (Agricultural Handbook no. 8-1, 1976); the British Medical Research Council's *The Composition of Foods* by R. A. McCance and E. M. Widdowson (1973); and *Manual of Nutrition* prepared by HMH Ministry of Agriculture, Fisheries and Foods.

My thanks go to Norman, Mallary and Amos Gelb for their help, cooperation, support and encouragement, without which I would never have been able to write this book.

I would also like to thank Diane Flanel of Paddington Press for her assistance in leading me safely and skillfully along the hectic paths of book publishing.

INTRODUCTION

We are what we eat. Fat, thin, imperfect or sublime, we are totally composed of ingredients derived from food.

Recent studies even indicate that our moods, mental attitudes and abilities may be influenced by our diets — scientists are still arguing about how. There is no doubt that our physical health and feeling of well-being is directly influenced by the nutritional content of the food we eat.

We must eat to live. We have no choice. Food gives us the energy to survive, to grow, to maintain and reproduce ourselves. We face continuing choices which are crucial to our well-being. "What shall I eat? How much? What will it do for/to me? The dietary decisions we make answering these questions are of great importance to each of us.

Despite the recent avalanche of literature on nutrition, most of us are still bewildered, left out in the cold, wondering how to understand its mysteries. Simple understandable explanations of what everyone should know about nutrition can be made. That is what this book is about. The answers can be found here.

The simple act of eating triggers a chain of complex happenings. Chemicals, aided by the grinding of our teeth, begin immediately to sort out and break down each mouthful of food. Very quickly, everything we eat or drink is reduced to its basic elements — proteins, carbohydrates, fats, fiber, minerals, vitamins and water. The proteins, carbohydrates, fats, minerals and vitamins are nutrients and are absorbed by our bodies to keep them functioning and growing. Excess amounts of the energy nutrients are stored as body fat — the more excess food we consume, the more weight we put on.

We can identify most of the nutrients in the food we eat. Each serves specific functions in the body. We know about most of those functions, and that knowledge is the groundwork upon which rules for proper eating and special diets are constructed. It is the basis for weight-reducing and weight-gaining diets, convalescent diets, fad diets, crank diets and personally invented diets.

It may be, as the old proverb says, that "diet cures more than doctors." But this is *not* a diet book. It does contain information about various kinds of diets, but it concentrates primarily on presenting an easily understandable close-focus picture of most of the dishes we actually eat, what they do for us and how we can improve our diets for better health. It deals as well with some of the more commonly accepted food fallacies, beliefs and customs.

For example:

☐ Yogurt is simply curdled milk. It has no more nutritional content than the milk from which it was made. It contains no secrets of long life.

☐ Honey is excellent for providing quick energy for athletes and others who need it. Otherwise it is merely sugar in predigested form and has little nutritional value.

☐ There is no scientific evidence for the commonly held belief that oysters promote sexual potency. But foods containing the mineral zinc (like cheese) are necessary for masculine sexual activity.

☐ Despite the old "Popeye the Sailor Man" cartoon, the iron in spinach exists in a form that cannot be absorbed by the body. However, in addition to being rich in vitamins, spinach is an excellent laxative.

☐ The best cuts of meat — choice, tender, succulent — have more fat and less protein and are of less food value than tough "jaw-breaking" cuts.

☐ One variety of a certain food may be more nourishing than another. For example, red peppers have far more vitamin A and C than green peppers. Cantaloupe melons have more vitamin A than other types of melons.

Cooking can seriously change the nutritional content of foods.

There is no point in buying an uncooked food rich in vitamins or minerals and then losing them when the food is cooked. Contrary to popular belief:

☐ Steaming food may not serve to retain its vitamin C.

☐ Vitamin C and potassium can be retained in certain foods if they are deep fried.

☐ Frying can triple the calorie content of some foods.

☐ Carrots keep their vitamin A when boiled.

☐ Fat may be absorbed into meat when it is being roasted, raising both the calorie and saturated fat levels.

Clearly, by knowing how to cook different foods, you will be able to include more nutrients in your diet.

For health purposes, everyone's diet must contain a certain minimum amount of nutrients. Carbohydrates and fats provide the body with energy and are stored as fat. Protein provides the materials for growth and repair of body tissue. It can also be used to provide energy. Minerals provide the materials for repair and growth of the body and for the substances of our bones and teeth. Vitamins help regulate body processes.

Minimum daily nutrient requirements vary from person to person according to age, size, general activity and other related factors, including the level of nutrition to which one has grown accustomed. Health departments of most large nations have drawn up minimum daily requirement charts which their health authorities think essential for their populations. The differences in their respective tables reflect different evaluations of nutritional needs. Two such tables are reproduced in this book: the Recommended Daily Dietary Allowances (RDA), prepared under the auspices of the Food and Nutrition Board of the National Research Council in the United States; and the Minimum Daily Requirements (MDR) established by the U.S. Department of Agriculture.

It should be borne in mind that the tables list only *recommended* minimum daily nutritional requirements. They should serve only as guides. No harm is done if a person takes a little more than the prescribed amount of a nutrient one day and a little less the next. Over a period of seven days, we usually adjust appetites to match our energy requirements.

Diets have become wildly controversial. Some nutritionists strongly praise certain diets which other nutritionists denounce as dangerous frauds. The best diet is one which helps a person feel healthy and well at a constant weight close to the weight prescribed for his or her age and body build. More activity than usual requires more energy and therefore more energy-giving foods than usual. So do pregnancy and breast-feeding. When the body is growing or recovering from injury it needs more protein, carbohydrates, minerals and certain vitamins.

It is the purpose of this book to make it possible for any person to determine, quickly and clearly, which of the foods commonly eaten will provide the nutrients needed for his or her specific purpose. When it comes to food, health does not have to be a mystery. It does not have to be expensive. It does not even have to mean a major change in diet. But it does mean knowing what the food we eat consists of, and that is what this book is all about.

WHAT'S IN IT FOR YOU
How to use this book

The Dictionary of Food consists of two main sections: "The Eater's Digest — A basic guide to nutrition" and "The Dictionary of Food."

THE EATER'S DIGEST
"The Eater's Digest" contains concise, clear explanations of various nutritional terms that appear over and over again in "The Dictionary of Food" section: calories; joules (the unit of measurement that is now replacing calories); proteins; carbohydrates; cholesterol; fats; minerals; vitamins; and water. You can find out where the discussion of each nutrient begins by consulting the "Page Guide to the Eater's Digest" on p.18.

Each of these nutritional elements have a separate section devoted to them to explain and clarify the role they play in our bodies: why each nutrient is important; what happens if our diets contain too little or too much of that nutrient; how we can ensure that we receive maximum benefit from that nutrient. In addition, each section contains a list of foods that are particularly rich in that nutrient, plus tips on how to cook various foods to retain their maximum nutritional value.

At the end of most of the sections are two tables which can serve as guidelines to the amounts of each nutritional element we should include in our daily diet: the Recommended Daily Dietary Allowances (RDA), prepared under the auspices of the Food and Nutrition Board of the National Research Council in the United States; and the Minimum Daily Requirements (MDR) established by the U.S. Department of Agriculture.

Although established by reasonable and responsible

authorities, the two sets of figures are at times at odds with each other. Both have been criticized. The Recommended Daily Dietary Allowances have been taken to task in some quarters for recommending figures that are too high. The Minimum Daily Requirements have been criticized for being too general and too limited: they prescribe limits for fewer nutritional elements than the Recommended Daily Dietary Allowances do, and they do not take as close a look at the changing nutritional needs of the body as it grows older.

Whatever the criticisms, the figures can be used as a useful guide to indicate how much of each nutrient our bodies require. The figures should be used as a guide only.

THE DICTIONARY OF FOOD

"The Dictionary of Food" consists of more than 180 main entries, each of which is broken down into two major parts: the Nutritional Content Tables and the notes.

The Nutritional Content Tables

The title at the head of each entry indicates the type of food described, how it has been prepared and its weight, which is normally given in amounts of 100 grams (3½ ounces) or 28.5 grams (1 ounce).

The amount of each nutrient present in a 100-gram sample also represents the percentage of that nutrient present in any quantity of that food. For example, there are 20 grams of protein in 100 grams of porterhouse, so 20% of any size serving of porterhouse steak is protein.

In the left column of each table is a list of nutrients. In the right column is a listing of the amount of each nutrient found in that particular food. If a food is especially rich in a particular nutrient, that nutrient will be marked with a star (✹).

The first two entries in the left column of the table are calories and joules, both of which measure the energy potential of a food. Following are proteins, carbohydrates, fats, cholesterol and fiber, all of which are tabulated in grams (g). Fats are further subdivided into two major categories: saturated fats and unsaturated fats. (For a discussion of the importance of this subdivision, see "Fats," p.29.)

If you add up the gram weights of the main nutrients in each table — proteins, carbohydrates, fats — you will notice that

12

there is a great variation between the sum of these figures and the total weight of the portion being examined. The difference is the amount of water contained in that food. For example:

In 100g of cooked summer squash, the carbohydrate + protein + fat = 5g. 100g — 5g = 95g, which is the amount of water present in the cooked summer squash.

In 100g of broiled porterhouse steak, the carbohydrate + protein + fat = 73g. 100g — 73g = 27g, which is the amount of water present in a porterhouse steak.

Vitamins and minerals are measured in milligrams (mg), which are $1/1,000$ of a gram; in micrograms (mcg), which are $1/1,000,000$ of a gram; or in international units (iu), which are $1/40$ of a microgram. The last unit is used to measure the amount of vitamin A and D found in foods.

Sometimes there is a hyphen (-) opposite a nutrient. This means that there is no information about the presence of the nutrient in that food.

The word "trace" in the amount column means that there is an indication of the presence of the nutrient, but it is too minute to measure.

The Notes
At the side of the tables are notes relating to the food in the Nutritional Content Table. They contain facts we should know about the food: how to purchase it; how freezing, canning or drying affects it; and what happens in cooking or storing it. Also included are nutritional comments on similar foods and on products which contain the basic food.

When a particular food in the notes is compared to the food analyzed in the Nutritional Content Table and no figure appears for an essential nutrient, it means that that nutrient is present in roughly the same quantity in both foods.

A Note on the Data Used in the Dictionary
The figures used in the Nutritional Content Tables and the

notes are based on the references listed in the "Statistical References" section of the Bibliography.

Nothing in nature is identical: slight nutritional differences will occur in all similar fruits and vegetables. Even animals from the same herd will be very different. What is amazing is the fact that, in spite of these variations, the numberical data given in these sources frequently agreed with each other, presenting no problem as to what values should be cited in the tables and notes. Occasionally, however, radical variation did occur, and it was in these instances where a choice had to be made as to which figure to include. In all cases, it was decided to ensure the health of the readers by choosing the lowest figure. In that way readers who want to rely on this book can be confident that the data in all cases reflects the minimum quantity of a nutrient that is present in any food. Readers can thus be sure that they are never getting less of a nutrient than the amount specified in the table.

Ways to Use the Tables
The tables are a simple A-Z reference guide for analyzing foods and can be used to discover what nutrients are present in a dish. Those whose diet must contain a specific nutrient (such as iron, potassium, fiber, or a particular vitamin) or those whose diet should be free of certain substances (such as cholesterol, fat, carbohydrates or sodium) should consult the "Eater's Digest" section. There, under each nutritional element (carbohydrates, protein, etc.) will be found a listing of foods which are rich in that particular substance. By going to the proper table in the "Dictionary" section they will then find the specific amount that food contains. For example, those who require potassium in their diets need only look under "Potassium" in the "Mineral" section (p.35 of the "Eater's Digest") to find a list of potassium-rich foods (chocolate, avocadoes, winter squash, etc.). The Nutritional Content Tables for these foods in the "Dictionary" section will indicate the amount of potassium each contains.

A good way to check whether you and your family are maintaining a balanced diet is to draw up a chart listing the foods and the amounts you have eaten of them throughout the day. Then make a column for each nutrient. Look at the Nutritional Content Tables and list the amount of nutrients in each food in the proper column. Add up the total of each column

14

and compare them with the Recommended Daily Dietary Allowances and Minimum Daily Requirements shown in the charts for each nutrient in the "Eater's Digest." The comparison should show you what your diet may lack. It may also reveal that there are some nutrients that you are eating too much of which you may need to reduce or eliminate from your diet.

If you are on a diet that does not specify all the foods you should eat, the tables will be a great help. They will be a guide to filling out the nutritional gaps and making your diet more interesting. They will show you other foods that fit the requirements of the diet. If you make a chart of all the foods on your diet, you may find that you are ignoring important minerals or vitamins. By using the tables you should be able to find foods which contain them and which also fit your diet.

EATER'S DIGEST

A basic guide to nutrition

Page guide to
EATER'S DIGEST

CALORIES AND JOULES

> Agony is putting yourself on a 1,000-calorie-a-day diet.
> Would you feel better eating 4,200 joules a day?
> It *sounds* better, but is there a difference?

All foods contain potential energy which, when eaten and acted upon (digested) by the body will be released. There are two units which measure the amount of potential energy contained in a food: calories and joules.

The Calorie

Calories are a unit of measurement (like pounds or grams) which can tell us how much energy we can get from the food we eat. We know that:

□ The basic metabolism uses 1 calorie a minute for breathing, operating our internal organs, etc.

□ Walking up stairs uses up 9 calories a minute.

□ Sitting still uses up 1.4 calories a minute.

□ Standing still uses up 1.7 calories a minute.

There are two types of calories: the calorie (or small calorie) and the kilocalorie (or large calorie). The small calorie, which is used as a unit of measure in chemistry, is the amount of heat needed to raise the temperature of 1 gram of water by 1° Centigrade. Because it is too small a measurement to determine the amount of energy released when food is digested, nutritionists use the kilocalorie instead. A kilocalorie is the amount of energy required to raise the temperature of 1 kilogram of water by 1° Centigrade.

To make matters more confusing, the kilocalorie is usually called a calorie. When the term *calorie* is used in the Nutritional Content Tables and elsewhere in *The Dictionary of Food* it means *kilocalorie*.

Joules

The International System of Units (SI), which now replaces all other forms of the metric system, has rejected the calorie in favor of the joule, which is considered a more accurate measure.

The joule is named after the British scientist J. P. Joule, the man who discovered the relationship between heat energy and mechanical energy.

The term *joule* is defined as the amount of force necessary to accelerate the movement of a 1-kilogram mass per second per second (or per second squared). Like the calorie, the joule is too small a unit to use in food sciences. Kilojoules are used instead, but they are called joules for simplicity.

There are 4.2 joules (kilojoules) in every calorie (kilocalorie).

Although most countries over the next few years will be adopting joules instead of calories, both terms are used in *The Dictionary of Food* to avoid any confusion that may arise in the transitional phase.

The Caloric and Joule Content of a Food

The amount of calories or joules in a particular food can be determined by breaking the food down into individual nutrients. Every nutrient has a specific caloric and joule value:

> 1g of protein yields 4 calories (16.8 joules) of energy.
> 1oz of protein yields 112 calories (479 joules) of energy.
>
> 1g of fat yields 9 calories (38 joules) of energy.
> 1oz of fat yields 252 calories (1,058 joules) of energy.
>
> 1g of carbohydrates yields 4 calories (17 joules) of energy.
> 1oz of carbohydrates yields 112 calories (470 joules) of energy.
>
> 1g of alcohol yields 7 calories (29 joules) of energy.
> 1oz of alcohol yields 196 calories (470 joules) of energy.

That value is then multiplied by the amount of the nutrient present in the food: for example, if a food contains 2g of protein, the caloric (joule) content of the protein is 8 calories (33.6 joules). The caloric (joule) values of all the individual nutrients are then added together to get the total caloric value of the individual food. This is how the values of the foods listed below were determined.

> 1 slice of enriched white bread has 68 calories (286 joules).
> 3oz of potato chips (crisps) have 483 calories (2,029 joules).
> 1 cup of cornflakes has 96 calories (403 joules).
> 1 tablespoon of honey has 43 calories (181 joules).
> 1 tablespoon of sugar has 55 calories (231 joules).

The Body's Energy Needs

The amount of energy an individual needs will depend on many factors. Among these are: height, weight, rate of metabolism, the amount of activity a person normally engages in (and where), and the type of work or occupation.

The Recommended Daily Dietary Allowance chart reproduced below has set a reasonable standard for the recommended amount of energy units needed by different age groups. The chart is to be used only as a guide, of course. Any chart which is set out in such general terms cannot possibly take into account the individual differences of bone structure, metabolism, state of health, profession, etc.

	Age	Average Weight kg	lbs	Average Height cm	in	Calories	Joules
Infants	0-½	6	14	60	24	kg×117	kg×491
	½-1	9	20	71	28	kg×108	kg×454
Children	1-3	13	28	86	34	1,300	5,460
	4-6	20	44	110	44	1,800	7,560
	7-10	30	66	135	54	2,400	10,080
Males	11-14	44	97	158	63	2,800	11,760
	15-18	61	134	172	69	3,000	12,600
	19-22	67	147	172	69	3,000	12,600
	23-50	70	154	172	69	2,700	11,340
	51+	70	154	172	69	2,400	10,080
Females	11-14	44	97	155	62	2,400	10,080
	15-18	54	119	162	65	2,100	8,820
	19-22	58	128	162	65	2,100	8,820
	23-50	58	128	162	65	2,000	8,400
	51+	58	128	162	65	1,800	7,560
Pregnant females						2,400	10,080
Lactating females						2,600	10,920

Calories, Joules and Body Weight

Sometimes the food we eat contains more calories/joules than our bodies can actually use. When this occurs, the excess is converted into fat and stored in the body.

Every extra 3,500 calories (14,700 joules) is converted into 1 pound (0.45 kilograms) of body fat.

A low-calorie weight-reducing diet is designed to limit the amount we eat by cutting down our potential energy supply, preventing us from having extra calories to be stored as body fat. Such a diet may even be planned to create a situation in which we can reconvert and use up some of the energy stored in our body fat.

A high-calorie weight-gaining diet is based on the reverse principle: it is designed to provide unnecessary calories which will be converted into fat.

PROTEIN

Protein is essential to human life. It consists mostly of carbon, hydrogen, oxygen and nitrogen, and exists in all animal and vegetable matter. Without it, bodily growth would be impossible and life systems could not be maintained. It is the basis of protoplasm, the primary substance of the millions of microscopic cells of which our bodies are constructed.

There are different kinds of protein, formed from various combinations of more than twenty types of amino acids. These combinations link themselves into chemical chains, each of which is unique. Beef protein, for example, is different from bean protein which, in turn, is different from bread protein.

The digestive system breaks down proteins. The digestive juices separate the chains into individual amino acids, which then enter the bloodstream to be selected by the cells that need them for growth or repair — like machinery positioned along moving assembly lines, picking and extracting necessary parts as they flow by. Protein which is not used can be stored as fat or oxidized into energy. Every gram of protein used by the body will release 4 calories.

The human body can synthesize more than half of the amino acids. There are eight amino acids, however, which it cannot synthesize and which must be supplied by the diet; children require a further two.

Animal protein — meat, fish, fowl and dairy products — is known as "complete protein," because it provides all the essential amino acids.

Soybean is the only vegetable that contains complete protein. All other vegetables have "incomplete protein" — they lack some essential amino acids. The missing amino acids can be provided through careful meal planning. The amino acids in foods containing incomplete vegetable protein such as bread and peanut butter will, during the digestive process, exchange amino acids until the right proportions are achieved and the protein becomes complete. Similarly, the amino acids in a complete protein food like beef and an incomplete protein food like beans can exchange their amino acids and become complete. However, for the exchange to take place in both instances, the foods must be eaten at one sitting.

Quantity of protein can usually make up for quality. Though incomplete and having less protein per ounce than animal protein, a combination of different vegetable proteins eaten in large quantities can usually suffice. Vegetable protein is also generally far less expensive than animal protein. It is found in substantial amounts in cereals, beans, legumes, chick peas, black-eyed peas and nuts.

Excessive heat will destroy some protein in animal and vegetable matter. During the baking of bread, an amino acid found in wheat is partially eliminated. Cooked beans have less protein than dried beans.

Gluten

Gluten is a wheat protein. It is the elastic substance in hard wheat which helps the flour rise when baked, giving the bread a sponge-like texture. Gluten is used as an additive in so-called low-calorie (starch-reduced) breads which are often eaten by people on low-carbohydrate diets. These breads have less calories per slice — not because gluten is low in calories, but because the addition of gluten causes the bread to rise higher during the baking process thus giving each slice less substance.

People allergic to gluten should avoid all wheat products. It can irritate the lining of the intestines and cause severe digestive problems.

Recommended Daily Dietary Allowances for Protein

Children	1-3	23g
	4-6	30g
	7-10	36g
	11-14	44g
Males	15-22	54g
	23 & over	56g
Females	5-18	48g
	19 & over	46g
Pregnant females		76g
Lactating females		66g

No Minimum Daily Requirement has been established for protein.

3½oz (100g) of roasted rumpsteak have 23.6g protein.
3½oz (100g) of roasted chicken have 27.1g protein.
3½oz (100g) of canned soybeans have 9.0g protein.
3½oz (100g) of broiled cod have 28.5g protein.
1 med. chicken egg has 6.2g protein.

CARBOHYDRATES

Throughout history mankind has relied on carbohydrates in foods such as bread, potatoes, rice and corn as the the mainstay of his diet. We depend on carbohydrates to satisfy our hunger.

Carbohydrates are essentially energy foods. During the course of digestion they are gradually broken down into simple sugars such as glucose and are then absorbed into the bloodstream and carried along to the tissues where their energy is released. When the body's glucose level rises, the pancreas secretes insulin, a hormone which converts some of the extra glucose into the animal starch glycogen, which is then stored in the liver and muscles. The remaining excess is converted into body fat, which the body stores as a reserve. One gram of sugar or starch will give off 4 calories (17 joules) of energy when digested.

Diabetes is the inability to absorb glucose into the system because of a lack of insulin. (Glucose is instead secreted in the urine.) The symptoms are hunger, thirst, itchy skin and gradual weight loss. It may also lead to serious heart conditions. Diabetics must restrict the amount of sugar in their diets. A new diet based on plant roughage (beans and whole grain) has also proved successful in controlling diabetes (for a further discussion of this, see "Fiber," p.26).

Carbohydrates also help convert fat into energy. Unless accompanied by a carbohydrate, fat cannot be completely digested. A residue is left which produces physical discomfort.

When eaten with protein, carbohydrates ensure that protein is expended on body building, while the carbohydrates are directed at supplying energy — hence the advisability of eating meat and potatoes, bread and cheese, etc.

Athletic coaches now realize that while protein serves as a long-term body builder, carbohydrates and fats (in foods such as spaghetti, bacon, butter and honey) supply energy quickly. Before their matches, some British rugby players drink sweet sherry flips (a drink similar to eggnog), which provide them with energy from carbohydrates as well as from alcohol.

There are four types of carbohydrates: sugar, starch, fiber (cellulose) and pectin.

Sugar

There are a number of different types of sugar. All are sweet to the taste, dissolve in water and are digestible.

Glucose, a simple sugar, is found in ripe fruit, plant juices, honey and onions.

Fructose, also a simple sugar, is found in ripe fruit, plant juices and honey.

Sucrose is what we normally use as table sugar. A combination of fructose and glucose, it is refined from sugar beets and cane sugar. It can also be found in ripe fruit, honey, maple sugar, beetroot, parsnips, carrots, and such dried fruits as prunes, dates, currants and raisins.

Table sugar has been so thoroughly refined that it is almost pure carbohydrate, with only very slight traces of some minerals and vitamins. Easily digestible, it converts into glucose in the digestive system and is a good source of energy.

Lactose is an animal sugar found in all types of milk.

Maltose is a malt sugar made from barley grains.

Too much sugar in a diet is undesirable. Its sweetness makes food more palatable and tasty, seducing us away from healthier foods (those with more useful nutrients) and inducing us to overindulge. Overindulgence with sugar can irritate the mucous membrane of the stomach. It can promote tooth decay and obesity and also lead to gout.

Some doctors believe that large doses of sugar taken at one time can promote a condition called hypoglycaemia, which is marked by headaches, inner trembling and a feeling of anxiety, lack of concentration and undue fatigue.

Starch

Starch is an unsweet, insoluble plant carbohydrate. Unripe fruit contains starch, which is converted into sugar as the fruit ripens. Raw, starchy vegetables like potatoes, cereals, rice and beans are practically inedible and are virtually useless nutritionally until cooked: cooking softens and breaks down the starch content, transforming it into a substance which digestive juices can turn into soluble sugars.

Toast and bread crusts have been recommended to the ailing for centuries — and with good reason. They are more digestible than an ordinary slice of bread because their starch content has been changed to dextrin, an intermediate stage in the conversion of starch into glucose. Though toast and bread crusts require more chewing, they mix easily with saliva (the first digestive juice) and are more readily digested.

Fiber (Cellulose)

This carbohydrate has no nutritional value because we are unable to digest it. It provides a very important function, however, as it provides the bulk, or roughage, in our diet. Roughage stimulates the intestinal muscles, a vital step in the excretory process, and thus helps to prevent constipation.

Research has shown that by increasing the amount of fiber in our diet, we can also increase our protection against illnesses of the colon. It was discovered recently that the meager diet of some African tribes contained more than three times the roughage of diets in industrialized countries. Among these tribes there was almost no cancer of the colon, diverticulosis nor other serious illness of the lower colon. Research has also indicated that colonic diseases only developed widely when societies switched their diets to refined foods (white bread, white sugar, white rice, white flour).

High-fiber foods like bran and wholewheat bread may contain an amount of phytic acid, which unites with calcium or iron to create an insoluble, indigestible compound. If the phytic acid is not destroyed by heat during baking or cooking, or if it is not already combined with the calcium or iron present in that food, it may combine with the calcium or iron present in other foods eaten at the same time, thus cancelling out their value. During digestion, traces of phytic acid might also combine with calcium or iron stored in the body, rendering those useless as well.

Experiments have shown that plant roughage in guar gum (which is extracted from cluster beans and consumed as part of a low-fat diet based on beans and whole grains) can effectively reduce the long-term effects of diabetes. The gum slows the absorption of sugars from the bowels, reducing the level of sugar in the blood. It thus permits diabetics to cope with more sugar in their diets and to require less insulin. Dr. D. Jenkins, the man who pioneered this research, also believes that it can be a very effective reducing diet, beneficial to anyone who is overweight.

Fiber can be found in wholemeal flour, wholemeal bread, brown rice, wholemeal cereals, bran and bran products, green bean strings, fruits, nuts and the outer skin of fruits and vegetables.

By peeling fruits and vegetables, we throw away a lot of useful fiber. Cooking and eating those skins would add that fiber to our diet.

Pectin
Pectin is a complex carbohydrate found in apples and other fruits and in such roots as turnips. It is used as a jelling agent. It is believed that it has no direct nutritional value as a food.

Daily Carbohydrate Requirements
Individuals vary enormously in their energy needs, according to age, physical build, type of usual activity, etc. The amount of carbohydrates a person requires is related to the amount of energy he normally expends. In a balanced diet carbohydrates provide most of our energy requirements.

Authorities differ on the proportion of the daily diet that should consist of carbohydrates. Between one-fifth and one-half of the calories in the daily diet should be from carbohydrate sources — it is an amount that can be comfortably consumed without adding weight or reducing energy levels. (See the section on Calories and Joules, p.21, for additional information on recommended daily requirements.)

---

1 slice of enriched white bread has 13g carbohydrates.
1 cup of cornflakes has 21.3g carbohydrates.
1 tablespoon of granulated sugar has 14g carbohydrates.
1 tablespoon of honey has 12g carbohydrates.
3oz potato chips (crisps) have 43g carbohydrates.

CHOLESTEROL

Cholesterol is a waxy substance present in the blood, brain and other tissues of the body. Recent studies have shown that it is an essential and major component of the walls that surround every cell in the body and that it must be continually available.

Cholesterol is manufactured by the body in the liver and the adrenal glands, and is the starting material from which the body produces bile and steroid hormones, among other substances.

Most of the animal products that we eat contain cholesterol. When our diets are rich in saturated fats, we raise the amount of cholesterol in our body (see "Fats," p.29).

It is now believed that an increase in the levels of cholesterol in the body causes the arterial walls to thicken and become lined with fatty deposits, leading to atheroschlerosis and coronary heart disease.

Cholesterol may also crystallize in the gall bladder, forming gallstones.

According to *Hutchinson's Food and the Principles of Nutrition,* studies have shown that deficiency of vitamin B6 increases the amount of cholesterol in the body.

Cholesterol-rich foods include: milk, liver, cream, meat, eggs, all fried food and shell fish.

No Recommended Daily Dietary Allowances or Minimum Daily Requirements have been established for cholesterol.

½ cup of crabmeat has 62mg cholesterol
6 oysters have 45mg cholesterol
3oz (85.5g) of sweetbreads have 396mg cholesterol
1 large egg yolk has 250mg cholesterol
3oz (85.5g) of liver have 372mg cholesterol

FATS

Fats and oils (which are mostly fats in fluid form) are the most concentrated form of energy food. They also contain fat-soluble vitamins (A, D and E). Our bodies will only digest those fats and oils which are soluble. (Mineral oils cannot be made soluble and therefore have a laxative effect.)

When fats are digested, they supply 9 calories per gram (257 calories per ounce), more than twice as much as proteins or carbohydrates. Eaten alone, fats are the most slowly digested of the nutrients. In fact, without the presence of carbohydrates or proteins, fats cannot be completely digested; a residue is left, which produces headaches, general physical discomfort and loss of appetite.

During digestion, fats are absorbed in the intestines and broken down by pancreatic juices and bile into fatty acids and glycerol. Some will be used for energy; some for conversion into fatty padding wrapped around the internal organs; and some for storage as body fat.

Fats give off heat as well as energy when they are digested. In cold climates many people increase their fat consumption in winter, providing themselves with additional heat as well as energy. Eskimos consume large amounts in the form of whale blubber. During the cold Russian winters, the Cossacks were known to consume large lumps of butter before knocking back substantial drafts of vodka, deriving heat and energy from both.

People who engage in difficult physical labor or who play energetic games benefit from increased amounts of fat in their diets.

There are two broad types of fats: saturated fats and unsaturated. All fats contain both types. Fats are classified, however, as either saturated or unsaturated, depending upon which of the two types exists in the greater proportion.

Saturated fats tend to be solid and are mostly found in animal fats. (Coconut oil and palm oil are unique among vegetable oils in having large amounts of saturated fats.) They last a long time before going rancid. Saturated fats also contain cholesterol, the waxy substance which lines the walls of the arteries and contributes to coronary disease.

Unsaturated fats are usually liquid oils made from vegetables, nuts or seeds. They turn rancid easily. Unsaturated oils used for frying may change their nature and become saturated during cooking. Only unsaturated oils that contain vitamin E, which is an anti-oxident, will remain unsaturated. These oils are: soya oil, soybean oil and corn oil.

There are two kinds of unsaturated fats: monosaturated fats and polyunsaturated fats.

Monosaturated fats (oleic acid) do not have any cholesterol content, nor do they assist in the storage of cholesterol in the body. Two such oils are olive oil and peanut oil.

Polyunsaturated fats (linoleic acid) help the body get rid of newly formed cholesterol, keep the cholesterol level down, and reduce the cholesterol deposits in the walls of the arteries. Some of these oils are: cottonseed, soybean, sesame, corn and safflower.

The American Heart Association recommends that our diet never contains more than 35% fat: of which 10% should be saturated and 10% polyunsaturated.

1oz (28.5g) of butter has 0.9oz fat, of which 60% is saturated and about 3% unsaturated.

Milk has 3.7% fat, of which 2% is saturated and 1% monosaturated.

Corn oil is 100% fat, of which 15% is saturated, approx. 30% monosaturated and 53% polyunsaturated.

Soybean oil is 100% fat, of which 15% is saturated, 20% monosaturated and 52% polyunsaturated.

MINERALS

There are at least 19 minerals in our bodies. They help build our bones and our teeth, and can be found in every cell and in our bodily fluids — in blood, lymph and even perspiration. We need minerals to help release our life-sustaining energy. When we have less than we should, problems arise.

Minerals are inorganic matter. Most of the minerals we need are present in our normal diets. Vegetables and fruits absorb minerals from the soil in which they are grown, and these in turn are passed on to us when we eat them. We also get minerals from meat (animals obtain minerals in the same way we do) and from the liquids we drink.

Our bodies dispose of minerals by perspiring, crying, urinating and defecating, and we must constantly replace them.

Calcium and Phosphorus

Calcium unites with phosphorus to form the major ingredient of our bones and teeth. When a baby is born, its skeleton is soft cartilage. To transform this cartilage into strong bone, calcium, phosphorus and vitamin D are needed. If any of the three are lacking, an infant's bones will not be properly formed, and its teeth, when they emerge, may decay.

Calcium is also needed to help muscles function properly, and blood will not clot unless there is enough calcium in the bloodstream.

When calcium unites with oxalic acid or phytic acid (present in foods such as spinach and beets, bran and bean products), an insoluble compound is formed that cannot be absorbed by the body (see also "Fiber," p. 26).

Calcium can be found in all dairy foods (milk, cheese, butter, etc.); eggs; flour; bread; oatmeal; nuts; sesame seeds; soybeans; turnips; green vegetables; small fish with edible bones, such as sardines, canned salmon, whitebait; and hard water.

Recommended Daily Dietary Allowances for Calcium		
Infants	0-½	360mg
	½-1	540mg
Children	1-10	800mg
Males & females	11-18	1,200mg
	19 & over	800mg
Pregnant & lactating females		1,200mg

Minimum Daily Requirements for Calcium

Infants	0-1	(No value reported)
Males & females	1-18	750mg
	18 & over	750mg
Pregnant & lactating females		1,500mg

1 cup of milk has 313mg calcium.
1 cup of ice cream (10% butterfat) has 176mg calcium.
1 cup of creamed cottage cheese has 126mg calcium.

Phosphorus is found in our tissues and cells, and plays a part in the release of energy. It exists in almost all our foods, so it is unlikely that the body will suffer a shortage.

Significant amounts of phosphorus can be found in bran, wholewheat foods, dairy products, eggs, meat, peanuts and peanut products.

The Recommended Daily Dietary Allowances for phosphorus are the same as for calcium, except infants 0-½, 240mg; and ½-1, 400mg.

Iron

Just as we need oxygen to live, so our bodies need iron to service that oxygen. Iron is part of the hemoglobin in the red blood corpuscles which carry oxygen from the lungs to the tissues to oxidize the nutrients and thus provide energy. It is also present in muscle protein and in enzymes which assist the oxidation process.

Once iron is absorbed, it stays in our system a long time and is used over and over again. Red blood corpuscles have a life of about 120 days. At the end of that time, the corpuscles are broken up in the liver, and the iron in the hemoglobin is released and held there until used again in the manufacture of new red blood cells.

Despite such economy, the body still loses iron. It is lost when we bleed, in the remains of digestive juices which are excreted, and through general wear and tear. Women suffer greater iron loss than men because of menstruation and pregnancy.

32

Iron deficiency can result in anemia and should be treated immediately. Doctors will normally prescribe large doses of iron salts.

The healthy body will only absorb iron when it needs it; the rest is excreted. There are also foods in which the iron content is of no value to the body: iron combined with phytic acid or oxalic acid is insoluble and indigestible, and will simply pass through the body. The iron in spinach, for example, is unusable for this reason.

Iron in most iron-rich foods, however, will supply minimum bodily requirements.

A baby is born with enough iron stored in its liver to last six months. If breast-fed, it will derive some iron from its mother's milk. If bottle-fed with cow's milk, it gets very little iron. If not put on mixed feeding, a six-month-old bottle-fed baby may become anemic.

Foods which contain digestible iron are: liver, kidneys, egg yolk, almonds, raisins, meat generally, dark meat of chicken, shellfish, molasses, enriched flour products, potatoes, cabbage, curry powder, water.

Recommended Daily Dietary Allowances for Iron		
Infants	0-½	10mg
	½-3	15mg
Children	4-10	10mg
Males & females	11-18	18mg
Males	19 & over	10mg
Females	19-50	18mg
	51 & over	10mg
Pregnant females		36mg
Lactating females		18mg

Minimum Daily Requirements for Iron		
Children	1-6	7.5mg
	6-10	10mg
Males	11 & over	10mg
Females	11-50	10mg
Females	over 50	10mg
Pregnant & lactating females		15mg

> 3½oz (100g) of broiled liver has 8.8mg
> 3½oz (100g) of fresh beef has 4mg iron.
> 3½oz (100g) of corned beef has 9.8mg iron.
> 3½oz (100g) of dried apricots has 4mg iron.
> 3½oz (100g) of wholemeal bread has 3mg iron.

Sodium

Sodium is one of the two components of salt (sodium chloride). Table salt has other substances added to it to assure smooth pouring. (Sodium in the Nutritional Content Tables in this book indicates salt content of specific foods.)

All body fluids contain specific amounts of salt. Deficiency of salt will make it difficult to digest protein and retain necessary body fluids. It will also cause muscle cramps.

We normally get enough salt in our diets. Any excess is often harmlessly eliminated in urine or perspiration.

In warm weather we tend to need extra salt. Steel workers, miners and others who do heavy manual labor in warm climates require extra salt in their diets. Major armies all over the world automatically supply troops operating in warm climates with salt tablets to be taken regularly.

In a temperate climate the daily amount of salt needed is about 4g. The whole of this may be lost in three hours of exercise or strenuous labor on a hot day. We usually consume about 5-20g daily in our food.

Excessive salt in the diet, though harmless for some people, may in others lead to hypertension, high blood pressure, congestive heart failure, or edema (abnormal swelling). Sufferers are usually put on a low-sodium diets. Babies must not be fed too much salt as their kidneys are not capable of coping with an excess.

Salt is found in all salted, spiced or smoked meats and fish; all canned foods (these have a high salt content); beer; commercially produced breads, cakes and biscuits; powdered milk drinks; cocoa powder; canned tomato juice; cheese; mustard; candied peel; crystalized fruit; and peanut butter.

No Recommended Daily Dietary Allowances or Minimum Daily Requirements have been established for sodium.

Potassium

Potassium's function in the body is similar to that of sodium. The precise distribution of sodium in fluids outside the cells and potassium inside the cells regulates the amount of water the body contains. Too much fluid outside the cells produces dropsy and edema; too little encourages dehydration.

Potassium also assists in the absorption of energy by our cells. It can be found in the red blood cells and in muscles.

Like salt, potassium is water soluble and will be lost by boiling. Normal dietary intake of potassium should reflect the amount lost in urine each day (2-4g). Patients who suffer kidney failure and are on kidney machines must watch the amount of potassium and sodium in their diets. Too much can cause sudden heart attacks. Such people should not eat chocolate because of its high potassium content and must cook vegetables for a very long time to reduce the potassium content. Potassium deficiencies occur with diabetes, kwashkiorkor and in conditions that increase urination.

Researchers in both the United States and England have been working on a theory that a high salt and potassium diet will increase the possibility that a woman will give birth to a male baby, while a low salt and potassium diet will increase the likelihood that she will have a girl.

Among the foods which contain potassium are: chocolate, avocadoes, mushrooms, potatoes, winter squash, bananas, beef, cauliflower, nuts, yeast and prunes.

No Recommended Daily Dietary Allowances or Minimum Daily Requirements have been established for Potasssium.

3½oz (100g) of milk chocolate have 384mg potassium.
3½oz (100g) of avocado have 684mg potassium.
3½oz (100g) of banana have 370mg potassium.
3½oz (100g) raw mushrooms have 414mg potassium.

Trace Elements

These are minerals that are found in the body in very small amounts. It is said that only traces of them are detectable, hence the name "trace elements." They are believed to be essential for proper nutrition. Recent research indicates that some — among them zinc, fluorine and copper — may be present in the body in larger amounts than was earlier believed and have specific functions. Scientists have found it difficult to confirm, however, that some of the other trace elements are essential for nutrition.

NOTE: If either the Recommended Daily Dietary Allowances and/or Minimum Daily Requirements do not appear for a particular trace element in this section, it means that the figures have not been established.

Zinc enables the blood to carry and release carbon dioxide, and helps strengthen the outermost layer of our skin. Zinc deficiency leads to stunted growth and anemia. It can also be responsible for a man's inability to perform sexually, a problem which may be resolved by increasing the amount of zinc in the diet. Our bodies need about the same amount of zinc as of iron.

Zinc is found in cheese and other dairy products, eggs, liver, oysters, herring, sea weed and maple syrup.

Recommended Daily Dietary Allowances for Zinc		
Infants	0-½	3mg
	½-1	5mg
Children	1-10	10mg
Males & females	11 & over	15mg
Pregnant women		20mg
Lactating women		25mg

3½oz (100g) of most cheese have 2-4mg zinc.
1 cup of milk has 0.9mg zinc.
1 egg has 0.01mg zinc.

Fluorine is found in bones and teeth. A strong case has been made for adding fluorine to drinking water — one part to a million — to decrease the frequency of tooth decay in children. However, too much fluorine in water can cause "mottling," the development of brown and white spots, on teeth.

Fluorine is found in fish bones, tea and water. Many toothpastes now also contain it.

Magnesium helps form bones and teeth and is essential for normal metabolism. It is present in most foods, so there is little likelihood of deficiency.

Recommended Daily Dietary Allowances for Magnesium		
Infants	0-½	60mg
	½-1	70mg
Children	1-3	150mg
	4-6	200mg
	7-10	250mg
Males	11-14	350mg
	15-18	400mg
	19-20	350mg
Females	11 & over	300mg
Pregnant & lactating females		450mg

Copper exists in all living things. Its exact function in the body is unknown, but it is thought that it might assist in the oxidation of nutrients. "Wilson's disease" creates a condition that allows the body to accumulate copper. This leads to cirrhosis of the liver and various neurological disorders. Though the disease is hereditary, only a few people afflicted by it survive to the age of procreation.

Iodine is the essential ingredient of thyroxine, the substance secreted by the thyroid gland which controls physical and mental growth. Goiter (excessive growth of the thyroid gland) can result from iodine deficiency. Children of mothers with goiters are sometimes born with inactive thyroid glands, but this condition may be remedied through intake of animal thyroid. (The children, however, may be born deformed or retarded.) Iodized salt has been used to prevent goiters in areas where few locally available foods contain iodine.

Iodine is found in fish and shellfish, and in vegetables which are grown in soil containing iodine (particularly watercress and onions).

Recommended Daily Dietary Allowances for Iodine

Infants	0-½	35mcg
	½-1	45mcg
Children	1-3	60mcg
	4-6	80mcg
	7-10	110mcg
Males	11-14	130mcg
	15-18	150mcg
	19-20	140mcg
	23-50	130mcg
	51 & over	110mcg
Females	11-18	115mcg
	19-50	100mcg
	51 & over	80mcg
Pregnant females		125mcg
Lactating females		150mcg

Cobalt is essential nutritionally for it is a constituent of vitamin B12, which is required for red blood cell formation. The Minimum Daily Requirement is 0.043mcg. This minute amount can be the difference between illness and health.

Molybdenum is an ingredient of an enzyme used in the formation of uric acid. It may not be necessary for health.

Selenium is present in brewer's yeast, eggs, onions and garlic. Some European farmers have been said to feed onion and garlic to their animals to cure blood clots and other atheroschlerotic obstructions.

Selenium is known to interact with vitamin E. A new drug consisting of vitamin E and selenium is now being tested for use in cases of severe heart conditions. Selenium may also be important in preventing muscular dystrophy.

Chromium is necessary for the formation and utilization of insulin in the body. Research has indicated that it may aid in lowering cholesterol levels and thereby help prevent heart and circulatory illnesses which result from the build-up of fatty deposits. The source of chromium in the body is unknown; the body rejects it when it is taken in soluble pill form. Chromium yeast is now being tested in the hope that it will provide a digestible source.

Boron traces are found in urine.

Arsenic seems to have something to do with phosphates and body structure. Traces are found in urine.

Nickel may be related to pigmentation.

Sulfur is obtained in the diet from protein foods. It is used for body building.

VITAMINS

Found in varying proportions in most foods, vitamins are essential for regulating the normal growth and functioning of the body. Until the twentieth century they were unknown, but as the discovery of various vitamins accelerated there were found to be enough of them to cover half the alphabet — and more are still likely to be discovered.

Vitamins were labeled by letter to distinguish among them before their individual unique chemical compositions were fully understood. Now many of them are identified by the names of their main chemical ingredients — thiamine for vitamin B1, niacin for vitamin B3, etc. For purposes of simplicity, in this book we have adopted the old vitamin lettering system.

Our bodies cannot produce most of the vitamins that they require for health and well-being. These can only be obtained from the foods we eat.

Each vitamin plays a specific role in maintaining the processes of life, particularly such bodily functions as tissue repair, growth and energy production. No vitamin is capable of doing the work of another. Lack of any vitamin leads to ill health; extreme lack leads to disease; prolonged deficiency could be fatal.

Excessive amounts of water-soluble vitamins, like the B vitamins and vitamin C, will usually pass through the body and be eliminated in the urine; physical discomfort or illness may occur, but the effects are usually not serious. Excessive amounts of fat-soluble vitamins like A and D, however, have been known to be fatal at times (see "Vitamin A," below).

Vitamin A (Retinol)

Vitamin A is essential to the growth of children and has a variety of other functions as well. It protects the skin, the moist areas of the eye, the mucous membranes of the throat, the respiratory tract and the bronchial tubes. Excess vitamin A is stored in the liver until the body needs it.

Lack of vitamin A lowers our resistance to respiratory ailments, the common cold and various other illnesses. It can also impair vision and cause night blindness.

Vitamin A deficiencies take several months to develop. Taking excessive amounts can also be dangerous. There is at least one case on record of a man dying as a result of overdosing himself with vitamin A pills.

Vitamin A is found in animal foods (including meat, eggs and dairy products).

Fatty fish, like herring and mackerel, and fish liver oils (cod and halibut) contain vitamin A (the fish produce it from carotene found in the sea plankton they eat). Liver and kidneys are also rich in vitamin A.

Vitamin A is also produced in the body from carotene, a coloring agent found in fruit and vegetables. Carotene is found especially in yellow and orange fruits and vegetables such as carrots, yellow sweet potatoes, yellow squash, tomatoes and red peppers. In green vegetables, the deeper the green coloring, the higher the carotene content. Spinach, watercress and cabbage have a high carotene content. Consuming an excessive amount of carotene is not believed to be dangerous, but it will cause yellowing of the skin.

Dairy products contain more vitamin A if they are produced in the summer, because the grass on which cows feed has more carotene than at other times of the year.

Boiling, steaming or soaking food will not reduce its vitamin A content. Frying, however, does tend to lessen the vitamin A content. Fried fruits and vegetables may lose even more of their vitamin A content if not stored in air-tight containers.

3½oz (100g) of raw carrots have 11,000iu vitamin A.
3½oz (100g) of baked winter squash have 3,500iu of vitamin A.
3½oz (100g) of cantaloupe have 3,400iu of vitamin A.
8oz of milk have 307iu of vitamin A.
1 slice of Swiss or American cheese has 212iu vitamin A.

Recommended Daily Dietary Allowances for Vitamin A		
Infants	0-½	1,400iu
	½-3	2,000iu
Children	4-6	2,500iu
	7-10	3,300iu
Males	11 & over	5,000iu
Females	11 & over	4,000iu
Pregnant females		5,000iu
Lactating females		6,000iu

Minimum Daily Requirements for Vitamin A		
Infants	0-1	1,500iu
Children	1-11	3,000iu
Males &		
females	12 & over	4,000iu

The Vitamin B Complex

We know of eleven vitamins which, considered together, are called the vitamin B complex. Eight of these are known to be essential to human nutrition. It is these eight which are discussed in the following pages.

All of the B vitamins are soluble in water and are usually found in the same foods. None of them are stored in the body, and so our supply must be renewed daily.

Vitamin B1 (thiamine) controls the oxidation (burning) of glucose when the body is releasing energy. If there is not enough vitamin B1 in the system, the oxidation leaves a harmful residue of pyruvic acid which damages nerves.

Our bodies manufacture small amounts of vitamin B1, but we must obtain an additional amount from the foods we eat. Lack of vitamin B1 will slow the growth of children and can cause loss of appetite, depression, fatigue, indigestion, constipation, irritability and inflammation of the nerves.

Beri-beri, a disease of the nervous system, is caused by a severe deficiency of the vitamin. At one time the disease flourished in the Far East, where many people lived on a diet of polished white rice, from which all vitamins had been removed from the refining process.

It has been determined that there is a relationship between the amount of vitamin B1 our bodies need and the amount of calories we consume. We need 0.04 mg vitamin B1 for every 100 calories consumed.

Vitamin B1 exists in most foods, with the exception of fats and sugar. It can be found in significant amounts in whole grains; wholemeal and wholemeal products; oatmeal; dried brewer's yeast and yeast extract; legumes and various other beans; potatoes; nuts; lean meats; pork and bacon; liver; fish and fish roe; eggs and milk. Any enriched product will have a substantial amount of vitamin B1 added to it.

□ Potatoes boiled in their jackets lose only 10% of their vitamin B1 content. When peeled, they lose 25%.

□ When fruits and vegetables containing vitamin B1 are boiled, steamed or soaked, half their vitamin content is lost to the water.

□ Vitamin B1 is destroyed by high temperatures. Roasting or pressure cooking destroys 30-40% of the vitamin in meat.

□ Bicarbonate of soda, baking soda and baking powder destroy vitamin B1.

□ Any sulphite used as a preservative in sausages and canned meats will destroy the vitamin B1 in that product.

---

1 slice of enriched white bread has 0.07mg vitamin B1.
1 slice of wholewheat bread has 0.09mg vitamin B1.
½ cup of cooked brown rice has 0.07mg vitamin B1.
3oz (85.5g) of lean roast pork have 0.55mg vitamin B1.

Minimum Daily Requirements for Vitamin B1		
Infants	0-1	0.25mg
Children	1-6	0.50mg
	6-12	0.75mg
Males & females	over 12	1.00mg
Pregnant & lactating females		1.00mg

Recommended Daily Dietary Allowances for Vitamin B1

Infants	0-½	0.3mg
	½-1	0.5mg
Children	1-3	0.7mg
	4-6	0.9mg
	7-10	1.2mg
Males	11-14	1.4mg
	15-22	1.5mg
	23-50	1.4mg
	51 & over	1.2mg
Females	11-14	1.2mg
	15-22	1.1mg
	23 & over	1.0mg
Pregnant & lactating females		1.4mg

Vitamin B2 (riboflavin) is concerned with the utilization of nutrients and the production of energy in the body.

When there is insufficient vitamin B2 in the diet, the tongue will become sore and inflamed; cracks and sores will occur at the corner of the mouth; the cornea and the front of the eye will become misty, making sight difficult. Deficiency in a child will cause the child to stop growing.

Vitamin B2 is found in liver, meat, meat extract, beer, brewer's yeast, eggs, beans, nuts and dairy products (milk, cheese, etc.).

Vitamin B2 is destroyed by a combination of ultraviolet light and heat, but not by heat alone. Milk will lose its vitamin B2 if left standing in the sun. Frying, roasting and canning also cause loss of vitamin B2.

3½oz (100g) of broiled liver have 4mg vitamin B2.
8oz milk have 0.4mg vitamin B2.
1 slice of American cheese has 0.1mg vitamin B2.
3½oz (100g) of broiled hamburger have 0.18mg vitamin B2.

Recommended Daily Dietary Allowances for Vitamin B2

Infants	0-½	0.4mg
	½-1	0.6mg
Children	1-3	0.8mg
	4-6	1.1mg
	7-10	1.2mg
Males	11-14	1.5mg
	15-22	1.8mg
	23-50	1.6mg
	51 & over	1.5mg
Females	11-14	1.3mg
	15-22	1.4mg
	23-50	1.2mg
	51 & over	1.1mg
Pregnant females		1.7mg
Lactating females		1.9mg

Minimum Daily Requirements for Vitamin B2

Infants	0-1	0.6mg
Children	1-12	0.9mg
Males & females	12 & over	1.2mg
Pregnant & lactating females		1.2mg

Vitamin B3 (niacin, or nicotinic acid) assists in the release of energy in the body. Lack of the vitamin in a child's diet will cause the child to stop growing. Deficiency in both children and adults may also cause pellagra. The first symptom of pellagra is a bright-red, swollen, sore tongue. This is followed by dermatitis in which the hands, face and neck become red and sore. Diarrhea follows, then mental illness and dementia. Treatment with vitamin B3 will cure the disease.

Tryptophan, an amino acid present in meat and milk, can act like vitamin B3 in the body. It, too, can prevent and cure pellagra.

Most foods that contain vitamin B1 and B2 will contain vitamin B3. Brewer's yeast and yeast extract, liver, kidneys, bread (enriched white and wholewheat), peanuts, broad beans, potatoes and chocolate all contain substantial amounts of the vitamin. Cereals also contain vitamin B3 but in an indigestible form.

Very little vitamin B3 is lost or destroyed when foods containing the vitamin are cooked.

---

1 slice of enriched white bread has 0.7mg vitamin B3.
1 slice of wholewheat bread has 0.7mg vitamin B3.
8oz of milk has 0.2mg vitamin B3.
3½oz (100g) of fried beef liver have 16.5mg vitamin B3.
3½oz (100g) of roast chicken have 7.4mg vitamin B3.

Recommended Daily Dietary Allowances for Vitamin B3

Infants	0-½	5mg
	½-1	8mg
Children	1-3	9mg
	4-6	12mg
	7-10	16mg
Males	11-14	18mg
	15-22	20mg
	23-50	18mg
	51 & over	16mg
Females	11-14	14mg
	15-22	13mg
	23 & over	12mg
Pregnant & lactating females		15mg

Minimum Daily Requirements for Vitamin B3

Infants	0-1	(No value reported)
Children	1-6	5.0mg
	6-12	7.5mg
Males & females	12 & over	10.0mg
Pregnant & lactating females		10.0mg

Vitamin B6 (pridoxine) is necessary for growth. It is involved in various chemical reactions in the enzyme system, the conversion of protein, the formation of red blood cells and in the nervous system and the skin.

Extreme lack of the vitamin produces dermatitis and severe disorders of the nervous system. Deficiency in men may increase the amount of cholesterol in their blood and lead to a thickening and degeneration in the walls of the arteries. Deficiency in pregnant women may lead to tooth decay.

Vitamin B6 is present in bananas, peanuts, fish, liver, yeast, potatoes, prunes and raisins.

Cooking lessens the vitamin B6 content of a food by 20-50%.

3½oz (100g) banana have 0.3mg vitamin B6.
3½oz (100g) of prunes have 0.2mg vitamin B6.
3½oz (100g) of walnuts have 1.0mg vitamin B6.

Recommended Daily Dietary Allowances for Vitamin B6

Infants	0-½	0.3mg
	½-1	0.4mg
Children	1-3	0.6mg
	4-6	0.9mg
	7-10	1.2mg
Males & females	11-14	1.6mg
	15 & over	2.0mg
Pregnant & lactating females		2.5mg

No Minimum Daily Requirement for vitamin B6 has been established.

Vitamin B12 (cyanocobalamin) contains cobalt, which is necessary for the formation of red blood corpuscles (see "Minerals," p.38). It is also necessary for growth and cell metabolism; the prevention of various forms of anemia, including pernicious anemia; and the prevention of the degeneration of nerve cells, particularly in the spinal cord.

Vitamin B12 is found only in foods of animal origin: milk, meat, eggs and fish. Liver is a particularly rich source. Vegans (vegetarians whose diet omits *all* meat products, including eggs, milk and cheese) need to supplement their diets with vitamin B12 to prevent the development of lesions in the nervous system.

Cooking will decrease the amount of vitamin B12 in a food by 20-50%.

3½oz (100g) of beef liver have 80mcg vitamin B12.
3½oz (100g) of liverwurst have 10mcg vitamin B12.
3½oz (100g) of salami have 1mcg vitamin B12.
3½oz (100g) of fried chicken have 0.4mcg vitamin B12.

Recommended Daily Dietary Allowances for Vitamin B12

Infants	0-1	0.3mcg
Children	1-3	1.0mcg
	4-6	1.5mcg
	7-10	2.0mcg
Males & females	11 & over	3.0mcg
Pregnant & lactating females		4.0mcg

No Minimum Daily Requirement has been established for Vitamin B12.

Folic acid (folacin) is concerned with the synthesis of nucleo-proteins. Lack of folic acid may cause megoblastic anemia, sprue and other gastro-intestinal disturbances.

Doses of more than 0.1mg of folic acid contained in vitamin preparations are considered dangerous. In the United States such preparations may be bought only with a doctor's prescription.

Folic acid is found in liver, kidneys, meats, fruits and vegetables.

Cooking will decrease the folic content of meats by 80-90% and of fruits and vegetables by 70-100%.

Recommended Daily Dietary Allowances for Folic Acid

Infants	0-1	50mcg
Children	1-3	100mcg
	4-6	200mcg
	7-10	300mcg
Males & females	11 & over	400mcg
Pregnant females		800mcg
Lactating females		600mcg

No Minimum Daily Requirement has been established for folic acid.

3½oz (100g) of cooked beef liver have 290mcg folic acid.
3½oz (100g) of fresh, unpeeled pear have 2.3mcg folic acid.
3½oz (100g) of pecans have 19.5g folic acid.
3½oz (100g) of fresh pineapple have 5.9g folic acid.
3½oz (100g) of banana have 10.9mcg.

Pantothenic acid is essential for healthy skin, body growth and the production of antibodies, which fight against infection. It is also necessary for the conversion of fats and carbohydrates into energy.

Lack of pantothenic acid causes a feeling of physical discomfort and uneasiness, muscle cramps, "pins and needles" in the hands and feet, and lack of coordination.

Pantothenic acid is present in many foods. Green plants manufacture it and store it in their seed coats. Any normal diet will contain an adequate amount; only an unusual diet (such as cases of anorexia nervosa) will not have any.

Foods which are good sources of pantothenic acid are: liver, kidneys and other offal foods, milk, yeast, raw herring, raw mushrooms, egg yolk and cereals.

Neither Recommended Daily Dietary Allowances nor Minimum Daily Requirements have been established for pantothenic acid.

3½oz (100g) of raw mushrooms have 2mg pantothenic acid.
3½oz of fresh tomatoes have 0.05mg pantothenic acid.
3½oz (100g) of dried dates have 0.8mg pantothenic acid.
3½oz (100g) of raw herring have 1mg pantothenic acid.

Biotin

Biotin is necessary for healthy skin. It also plays a part in our enzyme system. Our bodies manufacture biotin in the intestine; it has not yet been established whether we must get additional biotin from our diets to insure good health.

Lack of the vitamin will cause the skin to have an ashen pallor; it will also lead to muscular pains, lassitude and loss of appetite. An injection of 150mcg of biotin is sufficient to stop these symptoms and cure the deficiency.

Raw egg whites contain avidin, a substance which inactivates biotin and, in large doses, could cause symptoms of illness. Cooked egg whites do not have this effect.

Biotin can be found in most vegetables, particularly beans, cauliflower and leeks; liver and kidneys; milk; cheddar cheese; eggs; canned salmon; raw oysters; bread (white and whole-wheat); raw oatmeal; and nuts.

Recommended Daily Dietary Allowances and Minimum Daily Requirements have not been established for biotin.

3½oz (100g) of canned salmon have 10mcg biotin.
3½oz (100g) of raw oysters have 10mcg biotin.
3½oz (100g) of raw egg yolk have 25mcg biotin.
3½oz (100g) of raw ox liver have 100mcg biotin.

Vitamin C (Ascorbic Acid)

Vitamin C is needed for a clear skin, good complexion, strong gums, teeth and bones, and general good health. It may also reduce the risk of catching the common cold.

Without the vitamin, the body's rate of growth slows, the skin becomes blotchy and muddy, the gums bleed, and cuts and other injuries heal more slowly. Scurvy (scorbutus) will develop if vitamin C is not added to the diet. The first signs are severe pains in the joints, infection of the hair follicles and sore gums. Then the teeth loosen, the skin starts looking bruised and the pains in the joints become intolerable. If the deprivation continues, the patient will die. Scurvy can easily be cured (and also prevented) by taking 10mg of vitamin C a day, the amount contained in one orange or one tomato.

Here are some basic facts about vitamin C:

□ Liver is the only meat that contains vitamin C.

□ Babies derive vitamin C from their mother's milk, but cow's milk has very little vitamin C.

□ Vitamin C is found in most fruits and vegetables. The sooner a fruit is eaten, the more vitamin C it will contain. Conversely, the longer a fruit or vegetable is stored, the less vitamin C it will contain.

□ Summer fruits and vegetables contain more vitamin C than fruits or vegetables produced in the fall and winter.

□ Dried peas, beans, legumes, nuts and cereals contain no vitamin C.

□ Bean sprouts grown from dried beans do contain vitamin C.

□ Cherries, plums, grapes, pears, apples, carrots, lettuce, celery and cucumber contain very little vitamin C.

□ A fresh fruit or vegetable contains more vitamin C than a cooked fruit or vegetable. Fruits, however, will not lose as much vitamin C as vegetables when cooked.

□ A bruised or damaged fruit or vegetable contains less vitamin C than an unblemished fruit or vegetable.

□ A fruit or vegetable sliced with a sharp knife and eaten immediately will contain more vitamin C than a grated or minced fruit or vegetable.

□ 25% of the vitamin C contained in fruits and vegetables is lost by freezing. However, frozen produce may contain as much or more than the amount found in similar "fresh" market products or in foods cooked at home. This will depend on how fresh the frozen fruit or vegetable was before freezing and how much vitamin C it originally contained.

□ Canned fruits and vegetables may contain as much vitamin C as home-cooked fruits and vegetables, if the canning process occurred as soon as the produce was gathered.

□ Professionally dehydrated (dried) foods will retain 25-30% of their vitamin C.

□ Heat will destroy 5% of the vitamin C content of a food.

□ Cooking will decrease the amount of vitamin C in a food by 50-80%.

□ Vegetables should be cooked in a pot with a lid in only ¼ of the amount of boiling water necessary to cover them. This will save 40% of the vitamin.

☐ Bicarbonate of soda added to vegetables during cooking will destroy the vitamin C content of the vegetables.

☐ To preserve maximum vitamin C content, sliced vegetables should be dropped into boiling water, never cold or lukewarm water. Cooking should be stopped as soon as the vegetables are tender, and the vegetables removed from the water immediately.

☐ Using the water the vegetables were cooked in for stock is a way of utilizing the "washed-out" vitamins, as these will be transferred to the dishes being made with the stock.

☐ Steaming will destroy the vitamin C content of a food. Vegetables placed in a steamer will take a while to reach the temperature of the steam. In the meantime, certain enzymes are activated in the vegetable that destroy its vitamin C.

☐ Keeping a vegetable warm after it has been cooked lessens its vitamin C content. There is a 25% loss of vitamin C within 15 minutes; after 90 minutes, the loss is 75%.

☐ Vegetables in a steamer tray in a restaurant will contain very little vitamin C.

☐ Jams contain large amounts of the vitamin C found in the original fruits from which they were made.

Vitamin C can be found in particularly significant quantities in citrus fruits (oranges, lemons, limes and grapefruits), red and green peppers, brussels sprouts, broccoli, parsley, cabbage, strawberries, blackcurrants, and many other fruits and vegetables.

Recommended Daily Dietary Allowances for Vitamin C		
Infants	0-1	35mg
Children	1-10	40mg
Males & females	11 & over	45mg
Pregnant females		60mg
Lactating females		80mg

Minimum Daily Requirements for Vitamin C		
Infants	0-1	10mg
Children	1-12	20mg
Males & females	12 & over	30mg
Pregnant & lactating females		30mg

1 orange has 66mg vitamin C.
8oz of fresh orange juice has 124mg vitamin C.
8oz of prepared frozen orange juice has 112mg vitamin C.
1 tomato has 45mg vitamin C.
1 red pepper has 148mg vitamin C.
1 green pepper has 95mg vitamin C.

Vitamin D (Calciferol)

Vitamin D is as necessary as calcium and phosphorous for the formation and growth of sound teeth and bones in babies and young children. Even unborn children need an adequate supply of these three bone-building elements. Adults require a small amount for maintenance and repair; excess vitamin D is stored in our body fat.

Rickets is a vitamin D deficiency found mainly in children. It causes the cartilage to remain soft, leading to bow legs, knock knees, protruding foreheads and ill-formed teeth. Pregnant and lactating women can suffer from osteomalacia, a type of rickets caused when the vitamin D, phosphorus and calcium stored in a woman's bones is passed along to the unborn or nursing child. Men occasionally suffer from delayed rickets.

With the aid of the sun's ultraviolet rays, our bodies manufacture vitamin D. There is a substance under the skin known as ergosterol which will change into vitamin D when exposed to the sun's rays or to ultraviolet rays from sunlamps. Dark-skinned peoples have trouble making their own vitamin D because the sun has greater difficulty penetrating their skin. This may explain many cases of rickets in Africa and India.

Artificial sunlight can irradiate food, changing the ergosterol in it to vitamin D. Some foods, like yogurt and margarine, are supplemented with vitamin D.

Vitamin D is frequently found in the same foods as vitamin A. Adequate supplies of the vitamin can be obtained from foods such as cod liver oil, halibut liver oil, fatty fish like herring, mackerel, sardines, salmon, butter, milk and cheese.

Vitamin D is not soluble in water, so is not lost by cooking in water. Nor is the vitamin destroyed by heat. It is fat soluble, however, and is therefore lost in frying.

It is possible to suffer from excessive amounts of vitamin D. Doting mothers frequently "overdose" their children on the principle that "if a little is good, a lot is better" — the result may be hypersensitive children. Excessive amounts of vitamin D in adults and children may lead to nausea, loss of appetite, possible kidney damage and insoluble salts being deposited in the tissues.

The Recommended Daily Dietary Allowances and the Minimum Daily Requirements are exactly the same: 400iu a day for all age groups.

---

1 teaspoon of cod liver oil has 414iu vitamin D.
1 tablespoon of margarine has 86iu vitamin D.
1 tablespoon of butter has 61iu vitamin D.
1oz (28.5g) of canned salmon has 143iu vitamin D.
1oz of herring has 257iu vitamin D.

Vitamin E (Tocopherol)
Vitamin E is a fat-soluble substance that helps in the prevention of heart and circulatory diseases. One of its specific functions is to prevent polyunsaturated fats from oxidizing before the body has a chance to benefit from them.

Vitamin E is thought to have other functions as well, but these have not been verified. For example, it has been used to help prevent the formation of blood clots in the veins of the legs and has also healed some cases of scar tissue.

The cosmetic industry maintains that vitamin E used externally and internally helps to keep the skin young, but this has not been proved conclusively.

We know that animals need vitamin E for their reproductive systems, but have not yet discovered whether humans do.

A new drug consisting of vitamin E and selenium (see

"Minerals,"p. 38) is now being tested for use in cases of severe heart conditions. The combination has been used successfully on animals.

Vitamin E can be found in wholewheat bread, 100% all-wheat flour, wheat germ, wheat germ oil, roasted peanuts, peanut oil, butter, cheese and milk (especially if produced in summer) and some types of fatty fish like canned mackerel. It is also found in corn oil, soya oil and cottonseed oil if they have not been overpurified.

Bleaching and processing destroy the vitamin. Freezing foods which contain it partially destroys the vitamin. Oils that have gone rancid no longer contain the vitamin.

Recommended Daily Dietary Allowances for Vitamin E		
Infants	0-½	4iu
	½-1	5iu
Children	1-3	7iu
	4-6	9iu
	7-10	10iu
Males	11-14	12iu
	15 & over	15iu
Females	11 & over	12iu
Pregnant & lactating females		15iu

No Minimum Daily Requirements have been established for vitamin E.

> 1 tablespoon of butter has 0.3mg vitamin E.
> 1 egg has 3mg vitamin E.
> 1oz (28.5g) of roasted peanuts has 7mg vitamin E.
> 1 sweet potato has 4mg vitamin E.
> 6oz (171g) of brown rice has 2.4mg vitamin E.
> 1 slice of wholewheat bread has 0.5mg vitamin E.
> 1 tablespoon of soya oil has 13mg of vitamin E.

Vitamin K
Vitamin K acts as a blood-coagulating agent and is essential for the healing of cuts and other wounds. It is manufactured in the

small intestines and our bodies need very little of it. Deficiency is rare in a healthy person.

Vitamin K is found in most green vegetables. The darker the color of the vegetable, the more vitamin K it contains. Cabbage, spinach, green peas and alfalfa sprouts are particularly rich in the vitamin. Fruits, nuts and cereals do not contain vitamin K.

The exact amounts of vitamin K required by the body have not yet been determined, nor the specific amounts of the vitamin present in individual foods.

WATER

Water constitutes three-quarters of our body substance. Though not properly a nutrient, it is essential for digestion as it helps us to absorb the food we eat. It also helps to cleanse the body by removing bodily waste. When the body releases energy, two of the by-products are carbon-dioxide (which we exhale) and water, which we lose when we perspire, urinate, defecate and breathe. We usually lose as much liquid as we drink.

All foods contain water in varying proportions (see p.13 for a discussion of how to determine the water content of a food from the Nutritional Content tables in the Dictionary section).

Carrots are 91% water.
Bananas are 76% water.
Watermelon is 93% water.
Roasted chicken (with flesh and skin) is 57% water.
Steamed scallops are 73% water.

THE
DICTIONARY
OF FOOD

Page guide to
THE DICTIONARY OF FOOD

Following is a concise listing of all the foods covered in "The Dictionary of Food" section. The main entries reflect the main headings of each page in the dictionary. The subentries indicate foods other than the main food that are discussed in the notes accompanying each entry.

For ease of comparison, Certain foods have been arranged under broad, general headings: cod, salmon and halibut, for example, are treated under FISH. Other such general categories are: BEEF; BERRIES; CHEESE; CHICKEN; DRINKS, ALCOHOLIC; NUTS.

It should also be noted that the entries and subentries below are general ones only, to be used as a guide to how the A-Z section is organized. The notes accompanying each of the main entries in the dictionary are actually far more detailed than the listing suggests; they analyze not only the foods listed, but different variations of those foods. For example, APRICOTS, a typical entry, covers the fruit in the following forms: fresh, sweetened frozen; dried; dehydrated; canned; and candied.

84 **Bran**
Bran flakes; *see also* Wheat bran
85 **Bread:** hard roll
soft roll; Brown & Serve
86 **Bread:** rye
pumpernickel
87 **Bread:** white
raisin; French; cracked wheat
88 **Bread:** wholewheat
Dried bread crumbs
89 **Breakfast cereals:** corn flakes
Rice Krispies; Grapenuts; oatmeal porridge; puffed wheat; shredded wheat
90 **Broccoli**
91 **Brussels sprouts**
92 **Buckwheat:** whole grains
Buckwheat flour, dark and light
93 **Butter:** salted
unsalted; butter oil (dehydrated butter)
94 **Cabbage**
coleslaw, Chinese (celery) cabbage
95 **Candy:** milk chocolate
bittersweet chocolate
96 **Carrots**
97 **Cauliflower**
98 **Celery**
Celeriac
99 **Cheese:** cheddar
parmesan and others
100 **Cheese:** American (processed)
American cheese food, spread
101 **Cheese:** blue or Roquefort
Other blue-mold cheeses; semi-hard cheeses (e.g., Munster, brick)
102 **Cheese:** Camembert
Brie, Coulommiers, Pont l'Eveque, Livarot
103 **Cheese:** cottage
farmer's, pot, ricotta, etc.
104 **Cheese:** cream (full-fat soft)
105 **Cheese:** Swiss (Emmenthal)
106 **Cheese:** Swiss (processed)
Swiss cheese food
107 **Cherries:** sweet
sour cherries
108 **Chicken:** fryer
109 **Chicken:** roaster
Capon

110 **Chicken:** hens and cocks (stewing);
111 **Coffee:** instant (water and powder)
112 **Coffee:** percolated
113 **Cookie (biscuit):** chocolate chip
vanilla sandwich; short-bread; brownies with nuts; etc.
114 **Corn:** kernels
on the cob; cornflour; corn-meal; corn muffin. For corn flakes, *see* Breakfast cereals
115 **Crab**
116 **Cream: light, table**
half & half; whipping cream; sour cream
117 **Cress**
watercress
118 **Cucumber**
119 **Dates**
120 **Drinks, alcoholic:** beer
121 **Drinks, alcoholic:** spirits
122 **Drinks, alcoholic:** table wines
123 **Drinks, nonalcoholic carbon-ated:** cola-type
Others (club soda, ginger ale, diet soda, etc.)
124 **Duck**
125 **Eggplant (aubergine)**
126 **Eggs**
127 **Endive**
escarole, chicory
128 **Farina**
129 **Fats and oils:** lard and other
animal cooking fats
suet, beef drippings, com-pound kitchen cooking fats
130 **Fats and oils:** vegetable cook-ing fats and oils
peanut, olive, safflower, etc.; salad dressing (lemon juice and olive oil). *See also* Salad dressing
131 **Fennel (finocchio)**
132 **Figs**
133 **Fish:** bass
134 **Fish:** cod
haddock; cod and haddock roe; cod liver oil
135 **Fish:** eel
136 **Fish:** flounder
137 **Fish:** halibut
138 **Fish:** herring
139 **Fish:** mackerel

140 **Fish**: salmon
141 **Fish**: sardines
142 **Fish**: swordfish
143 **Fish**: trout
144 **Fish**: tuna
145 **Fish**: fish sticks
146 **Goose**
       Foie gras (goose liver paté)
147 **Grapefruit**
       grapefruit juice; candied peel
148 **grapes**
       Grape juice
149 **Ham**
150 **Honey**
151 **Ice cream**: vanilla
       frozen custard; ice milk;
       water ice
152 **Kale**
153 **Kidney**: ox
       sheep's kidney
154 **Lamb and mutton**: leg of lamb
       (roast); leg of mutton
155 **Lamb and mutton**: lamb loin,
       chop; mutton chop
156 **Lamb and mutton**: lamb rib,
       chop
157 **Lamb**: roast shoulder of lamb
       mutton stewing meat
158 **Leeks**
159 **Lemon juice**
       lemonade concentrate
160 **Lettuce**: crisp varieties (ice-
       berg, etc.); cos and romaine;
       Boston and bibb-type
161 **Liver**: calf's
       lamb's; sheeps's; chicken;
       etc.
162 **Lobster**
       lobster paste; lobster salad;
       Lobster Newburg
163 **Macaroni and spaghetti**
164 **Malt**: dried
       malt extract
165 **Mangoes**
166 **Margarine**
167 **Melon**: cantaloupe
       casaba; honeydew; water-
       melon
168 **Milk**: fresh whole pasteurized
       skim; buttermilk; evapor-
       ated; dried
169 **Molasses**: blackstrap
       treacle
170 **Mushrooms**
171 **Mussels and clams**

172 **Nectarines**
173 **Noodles**
       chow mein noodles
174 **Nuts**: almonds
175 **Nuts**: Brazil (American
       chestnuts)
176 **Nuts**: cashews
177 **Nuts**: coconut
178 **Nuts**: hazel (filberts)
179 **Nuts**: peanuts
       peanut butter; peanut
       spread; defatted peanut
       flour; chocolate-coated;
       peanut brittle
180 **Nuts**: pecans
181 **Nuts**: pistachio
182 **Nuts**: walnuts
183 **Olives**
184 **Onions**
       onion flakes; scallions (spring
       onions)
185 **Orange**
       orange juice, drink; candied
       peel
186 **Oysters**
187 **Parsnips**
188 **Peaches**
       peach nectar
189 **Pears**
       pear nectar
190 **Peas**: green
       split peas; peas and carrots
191 **Peas**: mangetout or snowpeas
192 **Peppers**: green (sweet)
       red, pimento
193 **Persimmons**: japanese (kaki)
194 **Pickles (cucumbers)**: dill
       sour; bread and butter;
       sweet; sweet relish; sour
       relish
195 **Pineapple**
       pineapple juice; pineapple
       and orange drink
196 **Pizza**
197 **Plums**
198 **Popcorn**
199 **Pork**: leg (roasted)
200 **Pork**: loin chops (broiled)
201 **Pork**: roast loin, salted smoked
       loin
202 **Pork**: spareribs
203 **Potatoes**: baked
       scalloped, au gratin

60

204 **Potatoes:** boiled
mashed; dehydrated potato
flakes; dehydrated potato
granules
205 **Potatoes:** french fried
hash brown; potato chips
(crisps), sticks
206 **Potatoes:** sweet
207 **Pretzels**
208 **Prunes**
prune juice, whip
209 **Pudding:** chocolate (home-
made); vanilla
210 **Pumpkin**
211 **Rabbit**
212 **Radishes**
213 **Raisins**
214 **Rhubarb**
215 **Rice, all types:** white
unenriched; enriched;
instant; brown; Spanish rice;
rice pudding
216 **Salad dressing:** mayonnaise
French, blue or Roquefort,
Thousand Islands, Russian
217 **Salt, table**
sea salt
218 **Sauces:** white
onion; tartar; brown
219 **Sauerkraut**
220 **Sausage:** bologna (all meat)
mortadella; liverwurst;
smoked liverwurst
221 **Sausage:** frankfurter (all meat)
bockwurst; knackwurst
222 **Sausage:** salami
dried salami
223 **Scallops**
224 **Seaweed**
kelp; dulse; agar; etc.
225 **Shrimp**
shrimp paste
226 **Spinach**
227 **Squash:** summer
zucchini; cocozelle; scallop;
yellow-crooknecked
228 **Squash:** winter
acorn; butternut; hubbard
229 **Succotash (corn and lima beans)**
230 **Sugar (beet or cane):** granulated
castor; powdered (icing);
brown (demerara); maple
231 **Sweetbreads:** beef (yearling)
calf, lamb

232 **Syrups:** maple
cane; sogham; blended corn;
blended maple and corn;
golden
233 **Tangerines**
tangerine juice
234 **Tea:** brewed Indian
instant tea
235 **Tomatoes**
tomato juice; concentrate;
cocktail; puree; paste;
catsup; chilli
236 **Tongue:** beef
hog; lamb; calf
237 **Turkey:** roast
turkey pot pie
238 **Turnips**
turnips greens; swedes
239 **Turtle, green**
240 **Veal:** roast
241 **Veal:** stewed (flank)
foreshank; plate meat; chuck
meat
242 **Veal:** chop
243 **Veal:** cutlet
244 **Vinegar:** distilled
cider vinegar
245 **Waffles**
246 **Wheat bran:** crude
See also Bran
247 **Wheat flours:** all purpose
bread; cake; gluten; self-
raising
248 **Wheat germ:** crude
toasted wheat germ cereal
249 **Yeast, brewer's**
dried yeast tablets
250 **Yogurt**
251 **Zwieback**
Rusks

ABBREVIATIONS AND SYMBOLS USED

mcg = micrograms

mg = milligrams

g = grams

oz = ounces

j = joules = kilojoules

c = calories = kilocalories

sat. fats = saturated fats (fatty acids)

unsat. fats = unsaturated fats (fatty acids)

− = exact amount not yet established

✸= significant amount of nutrient is present

MEASUREMENTS

Metric Weights

1 gram	= 0.035 ounces
28.35 grams	= 1 ounce
100 grams	= 3½ ounces
114 grams	= 4 ounces (¼ pound)
226.78 grams	= 8 ounces (½ pound)
500 grams	= 1 pound 1½ ounces
1 kilogram	= 2.2 pounds

NOTE: All cooking measures used in this book are Standard American measures.

American vs. English Weights

1 American cup = 8 ounces; 1 British cup = 10 ounces

1 American ½ pint = 8 ounces; 1 British ½ pint = 10 ounces

1 American tablespoon = ¾ ounce; 1 British tablespoon = 1 ounce

Some Useful Weights and Measures (American)

1 pound	= 16 ounces
1 tablespoon	= 2 teaspoons
2 tablespoons	= 1 fluid ounce
4 tablespoons	= ¼ cup
16 tablespoons	= 1 cup = 8 fluid ounces = ½ pint
2 cups	= 1 pint
2 pints	= 1 quart

NUTRITIONAL CONTENT	
Joules	243.6
Calories	58
Proteins	0.2g
Carbohydrates	14.5g
Cholesterol	0
Fat	0.6g
Sat. fats	–
Unsat. fats	–
Fiber	1g

Minerals

Phosphorus	10mg
Calcium	7mg
Iron	0.3mg
Sodium	1mg
Potassium	110mg
Magnesium	8mg

Vitamins

A	90iu
B1	0.03mg
B2	0.02mg
B3	0.1mg
B6	0.03mg
B12	0
Folic Acid	0.5mcg
C	4mg
D	0
E	0.7mg

When an **apple** is peeled it loses half its vitamin A content.

Frozen apples have lost most of their vitamin A and potassium content.

Processed apples and apple products generally have far less vitamin A and C than raw apples.

Unsweetened applesauce or artificially sweetened applesauce has less calories than a fresh apple of equivalent weight, and less vitamins and minerals.

Sweetened applesauce is much more fattening, giving you the calories and carbohydrates of the sugar added to the apples.

Apple butter has three times the calories, carbohydrates and phosphorus of a fresh apple. It also has twice the calcium, iron, sodium and potassium, but no vitamin A.

APRICOTS

RAW

3 medium-sized/100g/3½oz

Sweetened **frozen apricots** have almost twice the calories, carbohydrates and sodium of fresh apricots. There are less vitamins and minerals, but still a large amount of vitamin A. Manufacturers tend to add vitamins to increase the food value.

Uncooked **dried apricots** are highly nutritious, having almost five times the "goodness" of fresh apricots. When cooked (without sugar), they have more calories and carbohydrates than fresh apricots, and even more vitamin A, though less of the other vitamins. The more sugar they are cooked with, the more calories and carbohydrates they will gain. They will still contain large amounts of vitamin A and smaller amounts of folic acid and vitamin B6.

Dehydrated apricots, cooked in water with sugar, have almost the same content as dried apricots cooked in the same way. However, they have the same vitamin A content as fresh apricots.

Canned apricots, in heavy syrup, have approx. the same calories and carbohydrates as cooked dried apricots, with a third less vitamin A.

Candied apricots are just fattening: they have seven times the calories and carbohydrates of fresh apricots, and only minute amounts of other elements.

NUTRITIONAL CONTENT	
Joules	214.2
Calories	51
Proteins	1g
Carbohydrates	12.8g
Cholesterol	0
✹ Fat	0.2g
Sat. fats	–
Unsat. fats	–
Fiber	0.6g
Minerals	
Phosphorus	23mg
Calcium	17mg
Iron	0.5mg
Sodium	1mg
✹ Potassium	281mg
Magnesium	12mg
Vitamins	
✹ A	2700iu
B1	0.03mg
B2	0.04mg
B3	0.6mg
B6	0.07mg
B12	0
✹ Folic Acid	2.5mcg
✹ C	10mg
D	0
E	0.5mg

NUTRITIONAL CONTENT

Joules	**84**
Calories	**20**
✴ Proteins	**2.2g**
Carbohydrates	**3.6g**
Cholesterol	**0**
✴ Fat	**0.2g**
Sat. fats	**–**
Unsat. fats	**–**
Fiber	**0.7g**

Minerals

Phosphorus	**50mg**
Calcium	**21mg**
Iron	**0.6mg**
Sodium	**1mg**
Potassium	**183mg**
Magnesium	**–**

Vitamins

✴ A	**900iu**
B1	**0.16mg**
✴ B2	**0.18mg**
B3	**1.4mg**
B6	**–**
B12	**–**
Folic Acid	**–**
✴ C	**26mg**
D	**0**
✴ E	**–**

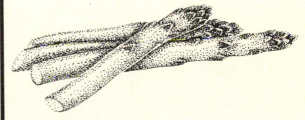

Canned asparagus (both green and white) is very salty, though special "diet" canned asparagus has very little salt. Otherwise it has the same value – somewhat less than that of fresh cooked asparagus.

Frozen asparagus, after cooking, has almost the same nutritional value as fresh cooked asparagus: there is slightly less vitamin A.

Both frozen and canned cooked asparagus contain a small quantity of vitamin B6.

AVOCADO
RAW
½ medium-sized/100g/3½oz

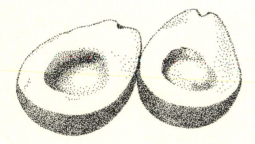

The **avocado** is sometimes called the alligator pear, and is native to tropical and subtropical America, where it was cultivated by the ancient Aztecs.

Nutritional content will differ according to the geographical area in which it was grown.

Because of its high fat and calorie content, it is frequently avoided on low-calorie diets.

NUTRITIONAL CONTENT	
Joules	701.4
Calories	167
Proteins	2.1g
Carbohydrates	6.3g
Cholesterol	0
Fat	16.4g
Sat. fats	3g
Unsat. fats	9g
Fiber	1.6g
Minerals	
Phosphorus	42mg
Calcium	10mg
Iron	0.6mg
Sodium	4mg
✴Potassium	604mg
Magnesium	45mg
Vitamins	
A	290iu
B1	0.11mg
B2	0.2mg
B3	1.6mg
B6	0.42mg
B12	0
✴Folic Acid	56.7mcg
✴C	14mg
D	0
E	1.2mg

BACON

CURED "STREAKY", BROILED OR FRIED, DRAINED
1 thick slice/12.5g/0.4oz

NUTRITIONAL CONTENT	
Joules	320.8
Calories	76.3
Proteins	3.8g
Carbohydrates	0.4g
✳ Cholesterol	11mg
✳ Fat	6.5g
Sat. fats	2.1g
Unsat. fats	3.8g
Fiber	0
Minerals	
Phosphorus	28mg
Calcium	1.8mg
Iron	0.4mg
✳ Sodium	127.6mg
✳ Potassium	29.5mg
Magnesium	3.13mg
Vitamins	
A	0
B1	0.06mg
✳ B2	0.04mg
✳ B3	0.65mg
B6	0.02mg
B12	trace
Folic Acid	0
C	0
D	0
E	0.06mg

Cured bacon is dipped or steeped in brine and then smoked.

Streaky bacon is the British name for bacon cut from the belly (underside) of a pig. It has all the qualities of a "fatty" meat: high in calories, fat and cholesterol and low in proteins.

Canadian (back) bacon is from the "eye" (inner section) of pork loin and is lean. It has half the calories, three times the sodium and twice the potassium of streaky bacon, and more cholesterol (2g per slice). When cooked it retains its salt, while cured bacon loses it in melted waste fat (a good reason for draining bacon while cooking it).

A thin slice of bacon weighs approx. 4g (1/16oz), and has 24 calories (100.8j), while a medium slice weighs approx. 6g and contains 36 calories (151.2j).

BANANA

RAW

1 small/100g/3½oz

NUTRITIONAL CONTENT	
Joules	357
Calories	85
Proteins	1.1g
✷ Carbohydrates	22.2g
Cholesterol	0
Fat	0.2g
Sat. fats	0
Unsat. fats	0
Fiber	0.5g
Minerals	
Phosphorus	26mg
Calcium	8mg
Iron	0.7mg
Sodium	1mg
✷ Potassium	370mg
Magnesium	33mg
Vitamins	
A	190iu
B1	0.05mg
B2	0.06mg
B3	0.7mg
B6	0.5mg
B12	0
✷ Folic Acid	10.9mcg
✷ C	10mg
D	0
E	0.4mg

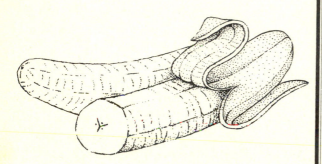

There are thirty known species of **banana**, and taste and nutritional content will vary slightly. The dwarf yellow and Canary Island red are considered to be the best tasting. Single bananas are called fingers, 8–12 fingers in a cluster are called a hand, and 6–18 hands are a stem.

Dried bananas have four times the nutritional value (except for a smaller vitamin C content) of fresh bananas.

A Hindu legend says that the banana was the forbidden fruit: when Adam and Eve lost their innocence they used banana leaves to cover themselves.

NUTRITIONAL CONTENT

Joules	105
Calories	25
Proteins	1.6g
Carbohydrates	5.4g
Cholesterol	0
Fat	0.2g
Sat. fats	–
Unsat. fats	–
Fiber	1g

Minerals

Phosphorus	37mg
Calcium	50mg
Iron	0.6mg
Sodium	4mg
Potassium	151mg
Magnesium	–

Vitamins

A	540iu
B1	0.07mg
B2	0.9mg
B3	0.5mg
B6	–
B12	–.
Folic Acid	–
✸ C	12mg
D	–
E	–

Yellow snap beans, green snap beans and **mung beans (beansprouts)** all have edible pods and are in the same family.

Yellow snap beans have the same food content as green snap beans.

Cooked frozen green and yellow beans are similar in nutritional value to their fresh cooked counterparts except for a loss in vitamin A.

Canned green and yellow beans have much salt, the amount depending upon the manufacturer. They are less nutritious, having fewer vitamins.

Cooked beansprouts have twice as much protein as green beans, but almost no vitamin A.

BEANS: white
BOILED AND DRAINED
100g/3½oz

NUTRITIONAL CONTENT	
Joules	495.6
Calories	118
✽ Proteins	7.8g
✽ Carbohydrates	21.2g
Cholesterol	0
Fat	0.6g
Sat. fats	–
Unsat. fats	–
✽ Fiber	1.5g
Minerals	
Phosphorus	148mg
Calcium	50mg
✽Iron	2.7mg
Sodium	7mg
✽Potassium	416mg
Magnesium	–
Vitamins	
A	trace
B1	0.14mg
B2	0.07mg
B3	0.7mg
B6	0
B12	0
Folic Acid	0
C	0
D	0
✽E	1.1mg

White beans, red beans, lentils, kidney beans, Windsor beans, chickpeas (garbanzos), cowpeas and **black-eyed peas** are all in the same family and all have similar nutritional contents.

They are recommended as a cheap source of protein — eaten in sufficient quantity they can provide enough protein for our daily requirements. They can also provide our daily requirement of potassium.

There is some question whether these beans contain the right proportions of the essential amino acids in the protein they provide. To ensure that you receive the proper complement of these acids it is suggested that small pieces of meat be added to a beans dish, as in chilli con carne or pork and beans (see *Proteins*, p.22).

Frozen and canned beans have a large amount of sodium. Canned beans tend to be poorer in nutrients.

NUTRITIONAL CONTENT

Joules	495.6
Calories	118
✱Proteins	9.8g
Carbohydrates	10.1g
Cholesterol	0
✱Fat	5.1g
Sat. fats	–
Unsat. fats	–
✱Fiber	1.4g

Minerals

Phosphorus	191mg
Calcium	60mg
✱Iron	2.5mg
Sodium	–
Potassium	–
Magnesium	–

Vitamins

A	660iu
✱B1	0.31mg
B2	0.13mg
B3	1.2mg
B6	–
B12	–
Folic Acid	–
✱C	17mg
D	–
E	–

Soybean belongs to the same family as the white bean. It is the richest and cheapest source of complete vegetable protein. It also has a high fat content and little starch. It is not very rich in vitamins.

Fermented soybean has one and a half times the protein of cooked soybean.

Fermented cereal and soybean has the same amount of protein as the cooked bean, but more than the daily requirement of potassium.

Soybean flour, the richest of all soybean products, contains four times the nutritive content of fresh cooked soybean, providing more calories and proteins as well as the daily requirement of calcium and potassium.

Soybean milk has one third of the protein of the cooked bean and half its calories.

71

BEEF: chuck from the arm

BRAISED OR POT ROASTED, 85% LEAN

100g/3½oz

NUTRITIONAL CONTENT	
Joules	1213.8
Calories	289
✱ Proteins	27.1g
Carbohydrates	0
✱ Cholesterol	77mg
✱ Fat	19.2g
Sat. fats	–
Unsat. fats	–
Fiber	0

Minerals

Phosphorus	134mg
Calcium	12mg
✱ Iron	3.4mg
Sodium	60mg
✱ Potassium	370mg
Magnesium	15mg

Vitamins

A	30iu
B1	0.05mg
B2	0.21mg
✱ B3	4.2mg
B6	0
B12	0
Folic Acid	–
C	0
D	0
E	0

When braising or pot roasting a piece of meat and a small amount of liquid are enclosed in an airtight container over a low flame. It is a highly effective method of tenderizing and flavoring meat. Any kind of meat can be braised.

Cooked chuck cut from the **fifth rib** (69% lean) has almost 50 percent more calories, 90 percent more fat and 20 percent less proteins. It has slightly less vitamin and mineral content. One study says that the meat contains 14.9mcg of folic acid.

Braised **flank steak** (mostly lean meat) has half the calories, 11 percent more proteins, only a third the amount of fat, and more vitamins and minerals.

Fatty meat has less proteins, minerals and vitamins than lean meats, and more calories, carbohydrates and fats.

BEEF: corned (salted)
BONELESS, COOKED, MEDIUM FAT
100g/3½oz

NUTRITIONAL CONTENT

Joules	1562.5
Calories	372
✳ Proteins	22.9g
Carbohydrates	0
✳ Cholesterol	77mg
✳ Fat	30.4g
Sat. fats	15g
Unsat. fats	13g
Fiber	0

Minerals
Phosphorus	93mg
Calcium	9mg
✳ Iron	2.9mg
✳ Sodium	1,740mg
Potassium	150mg
Magnesium	–

Vitamins
A	0
B1	0.02mg
B2	0.18mg
B3	1.5mg
B6	–
B12	–
Folic Acid	–
C	0
D	trace
E	–

Meat was pickled in brine, salted or smoked to preserve it in the Middle Ages. It would then keep for a long time in a cold place. Today, however, we pickle, salt or smoke simply for the flavor it adds to the meat.

A "noncommercial" pickle for meat would include:

1½lb salt (preferably sea salt)

8oz brown sugar

1oz saltpeter (potassium nitrate)

1gal water (or partially wine or cider)

The mixture is boiled, strained and left to cool. The meat is then immersed in it for a number of days, before being taken out to be cooked. Brisket of beef and chuck are two of the cuts of meat used for corned beef.

Commercial canned corn beef differs in content, taste and nutritional value, depending on the maker's recipe.

BEEF
HAMBURGER
100g/3½oz

A hamburger has as much protein as a steak of the same size, but is lower in calories and in fat.

The actual proportion of protein to fat will depend on the quality of the meat that goes into the meat grinder.

NUTRITIONAL CONTENT

Joules	1624.5
Calories	361
✱ Proteins	25.1g
✱ Carbohydrates	0
Cholesterol	77mg
✱ Fat	28.1g
Sat. fats	–
Unsat. fats	–
Fiber	0

Minerals

Phosphorus	125mg
Calcium	11mg
✱ Iron	3.3mg
Sodium	60mg
✱ Potassium	370mg
Magnesium	15mg

Vitamins

A	50iu
B1	0.05mg
✱ B2	0.2mg
✱ B3	3.9mg
B6	–
B12	–
Folic Acid	0
C	0
D	0
E	0

Any cut of meat can be stewed. Stewing is one of the most effective ways of tenderizing meat, which is why we associate it with the toughest (often the cheapest) cuts: short plate, rolled plate, plate boiling, shoulder, heel of round, shank knuckle, leg and neck.

Plate meat has a third more calories and twice as much fat as hindshank, but a fifth less proteins. The cholesterol content is the same. There is a slight variation in the minerals and vitamins.

Heel of round, shank knuckle and **leg** are all similar to hindshank.

Any food, liquid (other than water) or seasoning added to stewing meat increases its food value: if a medium onion is added to the meat, it will of course contribute its own nutrients.

Neck meat has a value similar to chuck meat.

BEEF: porterhouse steak

BROILED, 57% LEAN

200g/7oz

NUTRITIONAL CONTENT	
Joules	3906
Calories	930
✳ Proteins	39.4g
Carbohydrates	0
✳ Cholesterol	144mg
✳ Fat	84.4g
Sat. fats	–
Unsat. fats	–
Fiber	0
Minerals	
✳ Phosphorus	336mg
Calcium	18mg
✳ Iron	5.2mg
Sodium	120mg
✳ Potassium	740mg
Magnesium	42mg
Vitamins	
A	140iu
B1	0.12mg
✳ B2	0.36mg
✳ B3	8.4mg
B6	–
B12	–
Folic Acid	–
C	0
D	0
✳ E	1.2mg

Steaks have a large amount of "complete" protein: a half-pound of steak can give a person the recommended daily amount of necessary protein. But there is a correspondingly large amount of fat and cholesterol.

Porterhouse, T-bone, club and **hip-bone sirloin steaks** generally all have the same proportion of lean meat to fat and will offer the same nutrients. When cooked they have (in the examples studied) 58 percent lean meat to 42 percent fat. Though the figures may change, the steaks will offer similar percentages of nutrients as long as the proportion of fat to lean meat remains the same.

Porterhouse, T-bone and club steaks are all cut from the loin. Hip-bone sirloin steaks are cut from the sirloin (loin end).

NUTRITIONAL CONTENT

Joules	3696
Calories	880
✹ Proteins	39.8g
Carbohydrates	0
✹ Cholesterol	144mg
✹ Fat	78.8g
Sat. fats	–
Unsat. fats	–
Fiber	0

Minerals

✹ Phosphorus	372mg
Calcium	18mg
✹ Iron	5.2mg
Sodium	120mg
✹ Potassium	740mg
Magnesium	40mg

Vitamins

A	160iu
B1	0.1mg
✹ B2	0.3mg
✹ B3	7.2mg
B6	–
B12	–
Folic Acid	–
C	–
D	–
E	–

A piece of meat enclosed in an oven and cooked by a combination of hot air circulating around it and radiating heat coming from the walls is said to be roasted. In the old days, meat was roasted on a spit over an open fire.

Roast beef offers a large amount of protein. The amount of protein in a roast will depend on how much lean meat there is in relation to its fat.

A rump roast offers 25 percent protein. It also offers fewer calories than a rib roast and less fat (347c and 27g of fat).

The rib roasts vary slightly in calories, fats and proteins. Their contents depend upon which rib they are cut from. The sixth rib will have the highest amount of protein (20 percent of the serving), but only slightly fewer calories (3) and less fat. The eleventh–twelfth ribs will have more calories (40 more) and more fat than most of the ribs, but approximately the same amount of protein.

BEEF: sirloin steak

BROILED, 66% LEAN

200g/7oz

Meat placed on an open-work grill either under or over radiant heat is "broiled" or "grilled" when the outsides are browned. This dry quick cooking has a toughening effect on meat, so the meat must be tender and not too thick. If too thick the heat will not penetrate the meat adequately without burning the outsides.

Sirloin steaks have a large amount of complete protein. The leaner cuts — wedge and round-bone sirloin and double-bone sirloin steaks — have approx. 72 percent lean meat to 28 percent fat when raw, and 67 percent lean meat to 33 percent fat when cooked. They have more protein than the fatter steaks like porterhouse, and less fat.

NUTRITIONAL CONTENT	
Joules	3250.8
Calories	774
✱ Proteins	46g
Carbohydrate	0
✱ Cholesterol	144mg
Fat	64g
Sat. fats	—
Unsat. fats	—
Fiber	0
Minerals	
✱ Phosphorus	382mg
Calcium	20mg
✱ Iron	5.8mg
Sodium	120mg
✱ Potassium	740mg
Magnesium	42mg
Vitamins	
A	100iu
B1	0.12mg
B2	0.36mg
✱ B3	9.4mg
B6	—
B12	—
Folic Acid	0
C	0
D	0
✱ E	1.2mg

NUTRITIONAL CONTENT

Joules	134.4
Calories	32
Proteins	1.1g
Carbohydrates	7.2g
Cholesterol	0
Fat	0.1g
Sat. fats	–
Unsat. fats	–
✱ Fiber	0.8g

Minerals

Phosphorus	23mg
Calcium	14mg
Iron	0.5mg
Sodium	43mg
✱ Potassium	208mg
Magnesium	25mg

Vitamins

A	20iu
B1	0.03mg
B2	0.04mg
B3	0.3mg
B6	–
B12	–
Folic Acid	–
C	6mg
D	–
E	–

Both the beet and its foliage are edible.

Fresh cooked **beet greens** have a large amount of vitamin A (5,100iu) and calcium (99mg).

Canned beets have a great deal of salt, though special "dietary" canned beets have the same amount of salt as fresh cooked beets.

BERRIES: blackcurrants

RAW

100g/3½oz

NUTRITIONAL CONTENT	
Joules	226.8
Calories	54
Proteins	1.7g
Carbohydrates	13.1g
Cholesterol	0
Fat	0.1g
Sat. fats	–
Unsat. fats	–
✴ Fiber	2.4g
Minerals	
Phosphorus	40mg
Calcium	60mg
Iron	1.1mg
Sodium	3mg
✴ Potassium	372mg
Magnesium	–
Vitamins	
A	230iu
B1	0.05mg
B2	0.05mg
B3	0.3mg
B6	0.066mg
B12	0
Folic Acid	–
✴ C	200mg
✴ D	1mg
E	–

Blackcurrants, redcurrants, whitecurrants and **gooseberries** are all in the same botanical family, the *ribes* group. Their production and shipment is restricted in the U.S. by federal and state regulation, to stop the spread of white pine blister rust which uses these plants as alternative hosts.

Blackcurrants have a high vitamin and calcium content. In Britain and European countries they are much used as an alternative to citrus fruits as a source of vitamin C.

Redcurrants and **whitecurrants** have a similar energy-producing content (50c, 1.4g of protein, 12.1g of carbohydrates), much less vitamin C (41mg) and half the calcium.

Jam made from currants will have a much higher energy-producing content (from the sugar) and will have a somewhat lesser vitamin and mineral content. Some of the water-soluble vitamins and minerals will have evaporated slightly in the steam of cooking and will therefore be less evident in the jam.

Gooseberries have fewer calories (39c, 163.8j), proteins (9.7g) and carbohydrates (9.7g), and generally have only one third of the other nutrients found in blackcurrants.

NUTRITIONAL CONTENT

Joules	260.4
Calories	62
Proteins	0.7g
Carbohydrates	15.3g
Cholesterol	0
Fat	0.5g
Sat. fats	–
Unsat. fats	–
✳ Fiber	1.5g

Minerals
Phosphorus	13mg
Calcium	15mg
Iron	1mg
Sodium	1mg
Potassium	81mg
Magnesium	6mg

Vitamins
A	100iu
B1	0.03mg
B2	0.06mg
B3	0.5mg
B6	0.067mg
B12	0
Folic Acid	7.6mcg
✳ C	14mg
D	0
E	0

Blueberries and **cranberries** are single berries with small seeds.

Canned blueberries in heavy syrup become much sweeter and more fattening (101c and 26g of carbohydrates). They have lost half of the original fresh berry vitamin content.

Frozen blueberries lose half their vitamin C and some of their vitamin A content. Otherwise they retain their similarity to fresh blueberries.

Cranberries are much less sweet and have fewer calories (46c), less protein (0.4g) and less carbohydrates (10.8g). They also have fewer vitamins and minerals.

Strained sweetened cranberry sauce has all the additional calories (146) and carbohydrates (37.5g) that sugar adds, but even less vitamin and mineral content.

81

BERALES: red raspberries

RAW
100g/3½oz

Raspberries, blackberries, loganberries, dewberries, boysenberries and young berries are all similar. They are all clusters of little fruits, each holding a single seed, and they resemble each other nutritionally. There may be slight variations in their nutrients caused by soil, temperature and sunshine variation, and other uncontrollable factors. But in general, what will be true for the raspberry will be true for these other berries.

The **black raspberry** has more energy-producing nutrients: 73c, 1.5g of protein, 1.4 of fat, and 15.7g of carbohydrates. It has almost no vitamin A content.

Canned raspberries in heavy syrup gain calories and carbohydrates.

Canned raspberries without sugar or with only artificial sweeteners lose a third of their energy-producing nutrients, most of the vitamin C and half of the other vitamins and calcium of raw berries.

Frozen sweetened red raspberries have more calories than fresh berries (98), more carbohydrates (24.6g), and keep most of their vitamin C. The remaining vitamin content resembles that of canned raspberries.

82

NUTRITIONAL CONTENT	
Joules	239.4
Calories	57
Proteins	1.2g
Carbohydrates	13.6g
Cholesterol	–
Fat	0.5g
Sat. fats	–
Unsat. fats	–
✹ Fiber	3g
Minerals	
Phosphorus	22mg
Calcium	22mg
Iron	0.9mg
Sodium	1mg
Potassium	168mg
Magnesium	20mg
Vitamins	
A	130iu
B1	0.03mg
B2	0.09mg
B3	0.9mg
B6	0.09mg
B12	0
✹ Folic Acid	5mcg
✹ C	25mg
D	0
✹ E	4.5mg

NUTRITIONAL CONTENT

Joules	155.4
Calories	37
Proteins	0.7g
Carbohydrates	8.4g
Cholesterol	0
Fat	0.5g
Sat. fats	—
Unsat. fats	—
✹ Fiber	1.3g

Minerals

Phosphorus	21mg
Calcium	21mg
Iron	1mg
Sodium	1mg
Potassium	164mg
Magnesium	12mg

Vitamins

A	60iu
B1	0.03mg
B2	0.07mg
B3	0.6mg
B6	0.055mg
B12	0
✹ Folic Acid	4.6mcg
✹ C	59mg
D	0
E	0.2mg

A **strawberry** is not related to any other berry; in fact it is a member of the "Rose" family and is not a berry at all. That luscious red fleshy berry is really only the receptacle for the very small black seeds it bears – the real fruit.

Sweetened frozen strawberries have three times the calories (92) and three times the carbohydrates (23.5g), but lose a large portion of their calcium (13mg) and vitamin A (30iu).

When frozen strawberries are thawed their food value will be the same, but it will be distributed between the "berry" and the liquid juice.

Canned unsweetened strawberries have about a third less nutrients than fresh strawberries.

BRAN
WITH SUGAR AND MALT EXTRACT
100g/3½oz

NUTRITIONAL CONTENT	
Joules	1008
Calories	240
✸Proteins	12.6g
✸Carbohydrates	74.3g
Cholesterol	0
Fat	3g
Sat. fats	–
Unsat. fats	–
✸ Fiber	7.8g
Minerals	
✸Phosphorus	1176mg
Calcium	70mg
✸Iron	4-12mg
✸Sodium	1060mg
✸Potassium	1070mg
Magnesium	–
Vitamins	
A	0
B1	0.10mg
✸ B2	0.29mg
✸ B3	17.8mg
✸ B6	0.82mg
B12	0
✸Folic Acid	100mcg
C	trace
D	–
E	–

Bran is made from the outer layers of wheat grain. It has a large amount of fiber, potassium and the B vitamins.

Fiber is desirable in our diet because it acts as roughage and helps rid our bodies of waste products (see p.24). It will relieve constipation by making the stools softer. It can lessen the incidence of hemorrhoids.

It is now believed that an increase of roughage in our diet will lower the amounts of fats, calories, carbohydrates and proteins absorbed by the intestine, thus lowering the cholesterol in our bloodstreams.

Fiber has been used to relieve the symptoms of diverticular disease or irritable colon. One researcher believes that more fiber will lessen the incidence of cancer of the colon.

It is not advisable to include large amounts in the diets of the elderly or pregnant.

Bran with added sugar and defatted wheat germ has fewer calories (1.8), less salt (490mg) and less protein (10.8g), but it gains some vitamin B1 (28mg) and vitamin E.

Bran flakes with added thiamine (B1) have more calories (303), 2g less protein, 80.6g of carbohydrates and only 3.6g of fiber. They have an increase of vitamin B1 (0.4mg) but half the amount of the other B vitamins.

Bran flakes with added vitamin B1 and raisins have less calories (287), 8.3g of protein and less of everything else. The supplemented vitamin B1 is 32mg.

Always check the sugar content of bran products. Some manufacturers believe that the public prefers sweet products and have increased the amount of sugar they contain.

BREAD: hard roll
MADE WITH ENRICHED FLOUR
1 medium-sized, 3" across

NUTRITIONAL CONTENT

Joules	651
Calories	155
Proteins	4.9g
✴ Carbohydrates	29.7g
Cholesterol	0
Fat	1.6g
Sat. fats	—
Unsat. fats	—
Fiber	trace

Minerals

Phosphorus	46mg
Calcium	23mg
Iron	1.1mg
✴ Sodium	312mg
Potassium	48mg
Magnesium	—

Vitamins

A	trace
B1	0.13mg
B2	0.1mg
B3	1.3mg
B6	—
B12	—
Folic Acid	—
C	trace
D	—
E	—

Any roll made with plain flour which is unenriched contains less iron and vitamin B.

Hard rolls made with unenriched flour have less iron (0.4mg) and less B vitamins: vitamin B1,0.02mg; vitamin B2,0.04mg; vitamin B3,0.4mg.

Soft rolls of the same size have half the calories, protein and carbohydrates, and slightly more calcium.

Brown and Serve rolls are similar to soft rolls; they have 85 calories (357j), 2.3g protein, 1.6g fat, 15g carbohydrate and 21mg of calcium.

BREAD
RYE
1 medium slice/33g/1½oz

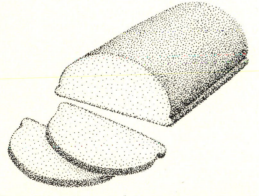

Rye bread usually consists of a mixture of rye flour and wheat flour. American-style rye bread contains one third rye flour and two thirds wheat flour.

Pumpernickel bread is made with very dark coarse unbolted rye mixed with wheat flour.

NUTRITIONAL CONTENT	
Joules	340.2
Calories	81
Proteins	3.03g
✱ Carbohydrates	17.33g
Cholesterol	0
Fat	0.37g
Sat. fats	–
Unsat. fats	–
✱ Fiber	0.13g
Minerals	
Phosphorus	49mg
Calcium	25mg
Iron	0.53mg
✱ Sodium	185.67mg
Potassium	48.33mg
✱ Magnesium	38.33mg
Vitamins	
A	0
B1	0.06mg
B2	0.02mg
B3	0.5mg
B6	0.03mg
B12	0
Folic Acid	5.2mcg
C	0
D	–
✱ E	0.8–1.1mg

BREAD

NUTRITIONAL CONTENT

Joules	378
Calories	90
Proteins	2.9g
✳ Carbohydrates	16.8g
Cholesterol	0
Fat	1.07g
Sat. fats	0.33g
Unsat. fats	0.67g
✳ Fiber	0.07g

Minerals

Phosphorus	32.3mg
Calcium	28mg
Iron	0.83mg
Sodium	169mg
Potassium	35mg
Magnesium	7.33mg

Vitamins

A	trace
B1	0.08mg
B2	0.07mg
B3	0.8mg
B6	–
B12	–
Folic Acid	–
C	trace
D	–
E	–

White bread is usually made from white wheat flours, yeast, water and/or milk. The flour is ground from the innermost starchy portion of the wheat grain.

It is "enriched" to replace many of the vitamins and minerals lost in the milling and purifying of the flour. All the B vitamins are added, plus iron and — if the additives to prevent spoiling do not already contain it — calcium. Vitamin D may also be added. Enriched white bread is similar to wholewheat bread in all ways except for its lack of fiber. All white bread manufactured in Britain is enriched.

Breads which are not "enriched" have the same calories, carbohydrates and fats, but will contain few vitamins and little iron or calcium.

Raisin bread is unenriched bread plus raisins (87 calories per slice).

French bread is made with milk, butter, flour, yeast and a large quantity of salt. It has more calories (96), more carbohydrates (18.4g) and more protein (3g) per slice. It also contains large amounts of sodium (27mg) and vitamin D. It is similar in other ways to unenriched breads.

Cracked wheat bread contains cracked wheat (wheat which is cut rather than ground) and all-purpose flour. It is like unenriched white bread but for its fiber content (0.2g).

The starch in toast and crusts has been changed to dextrin, making them more digestible than ordinary bread. For this reason they are usually fed to convalescents.

BREAD

WHOLEWHEAT, MADE WITH 2% NON-FAT DRIED MILK
1 medium slice/33g/1.2oz

Wholewheat bread is made from most of the wheat grain. It is rich in B vitamins and in vitamin E. It also contains a large amount of fiber which assists the healthy working of the bowels.

Dried bread crumbs are nutritionally similar to the bread they are made from, but will be richer in all the nutrients. They have lost their water content and ounce for ounce will have more concentrated goodness. There is a small amount of vitamin D present.

Despite baking, a small amount of phytic acid may remain in wholewheat bread. This would unite with an equal amount of iron and/or calcium to render it indigestible. Any acid left might well be capable of withdrawing some of the iron or calcium stored in the body. Some of the scientific community question the value of wholewheat bread in the diets of the elderly or pregnant since they are prone to calcium or iron deficiencies (see *Fiber*, p.26).

NUTRITIONAL CONTENT	
Joules	340.2
Calories	81
Proteins	3.5g
✸ Carbohydrates	15.9g
Cholesterol	0
Fat	1g
Sat. fats	0.3g
Unsat. fats	0.7g
✸ Fiber	0.5g
Minerals	
Phosphorus	76mg
✸ Calcium	33mg
Iron	0.8mg
✸ Sodium	175.7mg
Potassium	91mg
Magnesium	—
Vitamins	
A	trace
✸ B1	0.09mg
✸ B2	0.04mg
✸ B3	0.93mg
B6	—
B12	0
Folic Acid	—
C	trace
D	—
E	0.1mg

BREAKFAST CEREAL
CORN FLAKES (WITH ADDED NUTRIENTS)
100g/3½oz

NUTRITIONAL CONTENT

Joules	1541
Calories	367
Proteins	6.6g
✸ Carbohydrates	88.2g
Cholesterol	0
Fat	0.8g
Sat. fats	–
Unsat. fats	–
✸ Fiber	0.4g

Minerals

Phosphorus	58mg
Calcium	7.4mg
✸ Iron	2.8mg
✸ Sodium	1050mg
Potassium	114mg
Magnesium	16.5mg

Vitamins

A	0
✸ B1	0.43mg
B2	0.08mg
✸ B3	2.1mg
B6	0.065mg
B12	0
✸ Folic Acid	5.5mcg
C	0
D	–
E	–

Corn flakes were originally intended by their inventor, Dr. John Harvey Kellogg, to be eaten dry, and were produced as a health food for those with bad teeth and gums.

Rice Krispies have less nutrients than corn flakes. They have 351 calories (1471j), 6g protein, 1g fat and 85g carbohydrate. The mineral content is 144mg potassium, 128mg phosphorus, 799mg sodium, and only 0.7mg iron and 6.1mg calcium.

Grapenuts have 358 calories (1503j), 11g protein, 75g carbohydrate, 658mg sodium, 48mg calcium, 423mg potassium, 333mg phosphorus and only 5mg of iron.

Oatmeal porridge made with water (milk would be an additional source of nutrients) has far fewer calories and carbohydrates than the other cereals. It contains 45 calories (189j), 1.4g protein, 8g carbohydrate, 578mg sodium, 42mg potassium, and very little iron (0.4mg), phosphorus (43mg) and calcium (6.3mg). It contains 0.05mg vitamin B1, 0.01mg vitamin B2 and 0.1mg vitamin B3 as well.

Puffed Wheat has 358 calories (1503j), 14g protein, 2g fat and 75g carbohydrate. It has little sodium (5mg), 431mg potassium, 35mg calcium, 3mg iron, 35mg magnesium and 331mg of phosphorus.

Shredded Wheat has 362 calories (1520j), 10g protein, 78g carbohydrate, 3g fat, 16mg sodium, 4mg iron, 34mg calcium, 303mg potassium and 287mg of phosphorus.

Many cereal producers now add extra vitamins and minerals to their products, a move encouraged by various government bodies.

All these breakfast cereals are without added milk or sugar.

89

BROCCOLI
SPEARS, BOILED AND DRAINED
100g/3½oz

NUTRITIONAL CONTENT	
Joules	109.2
Calories	26
Proteins	3.1g
Carbohydrates	4.5g
Cholesterol	0
Fat	0.3g
Sat. fats	—
Unsat. fats	—
✹ Fiber	1.5g
Minerals	
Phosphorus	62mg
Calcium	88mg
Iron	0.8mg
Sodium	10mg
✹ Potassium	267mg
Magnesium	—
Vitamins	
✹ A	2500iu
B1	0.09mg
✹ B2	0.20mg
B3	0.8mg
B6	—
B12	—
Folic Acid	—
✹ C	90mg
D	—
E	—

Broccoli is a variety of cabbage grown for its immature flowers and flower stalks.

Frozen cooked broccoli is very similar to fresh cooked broccoli, but has slightly less vitamin C (73mg).

90

BRUSSELS SPROUTS
BOILED AND DRAINED
100g/3½oz

NUTRITIONAL CONTENT

Joules	151.2
Calories	36
Proteins	4.2g
Carbohydrates	6.4g
Cholesterol	0
Fat	0.4g
Sat. fats	–
Unsat. fats	–
✴Fiber	1.6g

Minerals

Phosphorus	72mg
Calcium	32mg
Iron	1.1mg
Sodium	10mg
✴Potassium	273mg
Magnesium	–

Vitamins

A	520iu
B1	0.08mg
B2	0.14mg
B3	0.8mg
B6	–
B12	–
Folic Acid	–
✴C	87mg
D	–
E	0.4 – 0.9mg

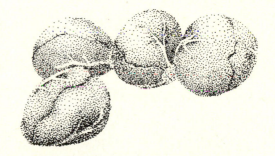

Brussels sprouts belong to the cabbage family. The plant grows its miniature "heads" along its stalk.

There is so little difference between fresh cooked Brussels sprouts and frozen cooked Brussels sprouts that they may be considered to be the same.

BUCKWHEAT
WHOLE-GRAINS
100g/3½oz

NUTRITIONAL CONTENT	
Joules	1407
Calories	335
Proteins	11.7g
✸ Carbohydrates	72.9g
Cholesterol	0
Fat	2.4g
Sat. fats	–
Unsat. fats	–
✸ Fiber	9.9g
Minerals	
✸ Phosphorus	282mg
✸ Calcium	114mg
✸ Iron	3.1mg
Sodium	–
✸ Potassium	448mg
✸ Magnesium	229mg
Vitamins	
A	0
✸ B1	0.6mg
B2	–
✸ B3	4.4mg
B6	–
B12	–
Folic Acid	–
C	0
D	–
E	–

There are two types of buckwheat flour: dark and light.

Dark buckwheat flour has the same calories, carbohydrates, proteins and fats as the whole grains. It has much less fiber (1.6g), less calcium (33mg) and no potassium. It has a high thiamine (B1) content (0.58mg), riboflavin (B2) (0.15mg) and niacin (B3) (2.9mg).

Light buckwheat flour has been refined. It therefore has almost no fiber and practically no B vitamins. It has half the protein and fat, but more calories (347) and carbohydrates (79.5mg).

NUTRITIONAL CONTENT

Joules	429.6
Calories	102.3
Proteins	trace
Carbohydrates	trace
✱ Cholesterol	31mg
✱ Fat	11.6mg
Sat. fats	7g
Unsat. fats	3.7g
Fiber	0

Minerals

Phosphorus	3.3mg
Calcium	3mg
Iron	0.02mg
✱ Sodium	117mg
Potassium	3.6mg
Magnesium	0.3mg

Vitamins

✱ A	434iu
B1	trace
B2	0.005mg
B3	0.006mg
B6	trace
B12	trace
Folic Acid	0.3mcg
C	0
✱ D	6iu
E	0.3mg

Butter is made by taking the fat content from milk and churning it until it reaches a solid state. Butter is known for its easily digested fat and for its vitamin A and D content. It has a large amount of cholesterol. It also contains traces of zinc.

Unsalted butter contains (per tablespoon) less than 1.4mg of salt (sodium) and potassium. All the other nutritional values are exactly the same as those of salted butter.

Butter oil or dehydrated butter has a large amount of calories (125), fat (14g) and vitamin A (583iu). It also has a large amount of vitamin D. It contains almost nothing of any other nutrient.

CABBAGE
RAW

100g/3½oz

Raw cabbage, cooked in water, will lose a portion
of its nutrients to the water. It does not matter how great
or little the amount of water is as the amount lost will be
approximately the same. A quarter of the calories will be
lost, and a very small amount of protein and carbohydrate.
The water-soluble vitamins and minerals will be reduced
the most. Vitamin C and most of the B vitamins will be
reduced by half. Vitamin B6 and folic acid will disappear.
Potassium, sodium and phosphorus will be reduced by one
third.

Coleslaw made from raw cabbage and either
mayonnaise or French dressing will have the nutrients of
raw cabbage plus those of the dressing (see *Salad
Dressing*, p216). The total amount of nutrients will depend
on how much dressing is used as well as the time of
serving. If the slaw is not served immediately much of the
dressing will be found in the bottom of the bowl, and its
nutrients will be lost to the salad.

The dressings mostly add calories, fats and sodium.
There may be a slight increase in the vitamin A content.

COLESLAW WITH:

	French dressing	Mayonnaise
Calories	129	95
Sodium	131mg	120mg
Fat	12.3mg	14g
Cholesterol	–	56mg
Potassium	197mg	199mg

Chinese cabbage or celery cabbage has fewer calories
(14), less carbohydrates (3g) and less fat (0.1g) than raw
cabbage. It has almost the same mineral and vitamin
content. It has only 25mg of vitamin C.

NUTRITIONAL CONTENT

Joules	100.8
Calories	24
Proteins	1.3g
Carbohydrates	5.4g
Cholesterol	0
Fat	0.2g
Sat. fats	–
Unsat. fats	–
✸ Fiber	0.8g

Minerals
Phosphorus	29mg
Calcium	49mg
Iron	0.4mg
Sodium	20mg
✸ Potassium	233mg
Magnesium	13mg

Vitamins
A	130iu
✸ B1	0.05mg
B2	0.05mg
✸ B3	0.3mg
B6	0.16mg
B12	0
✸ Folic Acid	6 – 42mcg
✸ C	47mg
D	0
E	0.1mg

NUTRITIONAL CONTENT

Joules	2184
Calories	520
Proteins	7.7g
✹ Carbohydrates	56.9g
Cholesterol	–
✹ Fat	32.3g
✹ Sat. fats	20g
Unsat. fats	14g
Fiber	0.4g

Minerals

Phosphorus	231mg
✹ Calcium	228mg
Iron	1.1mg
Sodium	94mg
✹ Potassium	384mg
✹ Magnesium	58mg

Vitamins

✹ A	2701iu
B1	0.06mg
B2	0.34
✹ B3	0.3mg
B6	–
B12	–
Folic Acid	–
C	trace
D	–
E	–

All chocolate is highly nutritious. It is high in calories, carbohydrates and fats. It also contains a large amount of potassium.

Bittersweet chocolate contains the highest amount of potassium (615mg) and, since it is less sweet, also contains fewer calories (477).

Milk chocolate contains a high portion of calcium and vitamin A. If nuts are added they displace some of the chocolate and substitute their own nutrients. Peanuts have a large amount of protein and potassium: adding them to milk chocolate gives 14g of protein and 487mg of potassium.

CARROTS
RAW

100g/3½oz

NUTRITIONAL CONTENT	
Joules	176.4
Calories	42
Proteins	1.1g
Carbohydrates	9.7g
Cholesterol	0
Fat	0.2g
Sat. fats	–
Unsat. fats	–
✷Fiber	1g
Minerals	
Phosphorus	36mg
Calcium	37mg
Iron	0.7mg
Sodium	47mg
✷Potassium	341mg
Magnesium	23mg
Vitamins	
✷A	11000iu
B1	0.06mg
B2	0.05mg
✷B3	0.6mg
B6	0.15mg
B12	0
✷Folic Acid	7.6mcg
C	8mg
D	0
✷E	0.5mg

Cooked carrots lose a portion of their nutrients when boiled and drained. They retain 31 calories and a very large portion of their vitamin A content (10,500iu). Their potassium content is reduced by one third to 222mg.

Canned carrots which are cooked have less nutrients than cooked fresh carrots. They still retain a large amount of vitamin A (10,000iu). They also have an enormous amount of salt (236mg).

Diet canned carrots are like canned carrots minus the salt. They have their salt content reduced to 39mg (less than fresh carrots).

NUTRITIONAL CONTENT	
Joules	92.4
Calories	22
Proteins	2.3g
Carbohydrates	4.1g
Cholesterol	0
Fat	0.2g
Sat. fats	–
Unsat. fats	–
✸ Fiber	1g

Minerals

Phosphorus	42mg
Calcium	21mg
Iron	0.7mg
Sodium	9mg
✸ Potassium	206mg
Magnesium	–

Vitamins

A	60iu
B1	0.09mg
B2	0.08mg
✸ B3	0.6mg
B6	–
B12	–
Folic Acid	–
✸ C	55mg
D	–
E	–

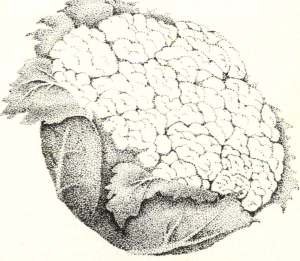

Cauliflower is a member of the cabbage family. The green leaves of the cauliflower will indicate its freshness.

Frozen cooked cauliflower loses more nutrients than freshly cooked cauliflower. It retains 18 calories, 1.9g protein, 3.3g carbohydrates and 17g calcium. Its small amount of vitamin content is reduced by about a third, but it does keep 41mg of vitamin C.

CELERY

RAW

100g/3½oz

NUTRITIONAL CONTENT	
Joules	71.4
Calories	17
Proteins	0.9g
Carbohydrates	3.9g
Cholesterol	0
Fat	0.1g
Sat. fats	—
Unsat. fats	—
✹ Fiber	0.6g
Minerals	
Phosphorus	29mg
Calcium	39mg
Iron	0.3mg
Sodium	126mg
✹ Potassium	341mg
Magnesium	—
Vitamins	
A	240iu
B1	0.03mg
B2	0.03mg
✹ B3	0.3mg
B6	0.06mg
B12	0
✹ Folic Acid	8.5mcg
C	9mg
D	0
E	0.5mg

Stem celery, which is the kind we most eat, comes from wild celery and was used by the early Romans.

Boiled and drained celery loses very few of the nutrients. For example, only 3 calories, 0.2g protein, 0.7g carbohydrates and a minimal amount of vitamins are lost.

Frozen cooked celery loses very little of its nutrients.

Celeriac is the celery plant developed for its edible root. It is the storehouse for the energy of the plant. It has a high caloric content (40 calories), and a high carbohydrate content (8.5g). It contains 1.8g of proteins. In its raw state it contains a large amount of sodium (100mg) and potassium (300mg) — almost as much as raw celery. Celeriac contains no vitamin A. The rest of its small amount of vitamins is similar to that of stem celery.

NUTRITIONAL CONTENT

Joules	1671.6
Calories	398
Proteins	25g
Carbohydrates	2.1g
✸Cholesterol	100mg
✸Fat	32.2g
Sat. fats	18g
Unsat. fats	12g
Fiber	0

Minerals

✸Phosphorus	478mg
✸Calcium	750mg
Iron	1mg
✸Sodium	700mg
Potassium	82mg
Magnesium	45mg

Vitamins

✸A	1310iu
B1	0.03mg
✸B2	0.46mg
B3	0.1mg
B6	0.08mg
✸B12	0.001mg
✸Folic Acid	12.4mcg
C	0
✸D	14iu
✸E	1 – 1.6mg

Cheddar cheese is a hard cheese. Like all hard cheeses, it is made from raw milk and is bacteria-ripened. It is aged from three to twelve months, and will retain 30 percent of its moisture after aging. Cheddar cheese has a large amount of protein, calories and cholesterol. It has a high fat content and is also rich in calcium, sodium and vitamin A. It is excellent for cooking, particularly if it is grated first. To prevent cheddar cheese going dry after cutting, one cookbook suggests buttering the cut edges before wrapping and refrigerating.

There are many kinds of hard cheeses, all having different aging periods:

2-3 months: Appitost, Nokkelost, Kuminnost
3-12 months: American, Asiago, Apple, Cheddar, Edam, Gjetost, Gruyère, Provolone, Sapsago, Sbrinz, Swiss
12-16 months: Cheshire, Parmesan, Romano, Sardo

Parmesan cheese has a similar nutritional content to Cheddar cheese. It is high in protein (36g), high in calories (393), has slightly less fat (26g), an enormous calcium content (1140mg), is high in sodium (742mg) and has a large vitamin A content (1060iu).

CHEESE

PASTEURIZED PROCESSED AMERICAN
100g/3½oz

Processed cheese, once described as "the triumph of technology over conscience" is a pasteurized, homogenized blend of new green cheeses and one or more aged cheeses, heated together with emulsifying salts and up to 3 percent water, and poured into loaf-shaped molds. It is a cheap and nourishing source of energy and proteins. Its nutritional content does not differ much from "natural" American cheese, but it does differ in its bland, uninteresting flavor and in its texture, as well as in its enormous salt content. Processed cheese can be stored indefinitely if refrigerated, which is of value to the shopkeeper as well as to the customer.

Pasteurized processed American cheese food is made in the same way, but can contain up to 40 percent water. Containing less of everything, it has 322 calories, 19.8g protein, 24g fat, 7g carbohydrates, 570mg calcium, a large amount of salt and 980iu vitamin A. (Its vitamin B content is the same as in processed cheese.)

Pasteurized processed American cheese spread can contain up to 60 percent water, gums and gelatins. It need not contain any cheese at all. It has a reasonably large supply of calories (288), proteins (16g), carbohydrates (8g) and fat (21g). It contains more than the daily requirement of calcium (565mg) and 875mg phosphorus. It too has an enormous salt content (1625mg), but less vitamin A than the other products.

Both of these products provide less nutrients than "natural" cheese, but they nevertheless provide substantial nourishment.

NUTRITIONAL CONTENT

Joules	1554
Calories	370
✳ Proteins	23.2g
Carbohydrates	1.9g
✳ Cholesterol	87mg
✳ Fat	30g
Sat. fats	18g
Unsat. fats	12g
Fiber	0

Minerals

✳ Phosphorus	771mg
✳ Calcium	697mg
Iron	0.9mg
✳ Sodium	1136mg
Potassium	80mg
Magnesium	45mg

Vitamins

✳ A	1220iu
B1	0.02mg
✳ B2	0.41mg
B3	trace
B6	0.08mg
B12	0.0008mg
✳ Folic Acid	11mcg
C	0
✳ D	12iu
✳ E	1mg

NUTRITIONAL CONTENT

Joules	1545.6
Calories	368
✸Proteins	21.5g
Carbohydrates	2g
✸Cholesterol	84mg
✸Fat	31.5g
✸ Sat. fats	17.5g
Unsat. fats	10.5g plus
Fiber	0

Minerals

Phosphorus	339mg
✸Calcium	315mg
Iron	0.5mg
Sodium	–
Potassium	–
Magnesium	–

Vitamins

✸A	1240iu
B1	0.03mg
✸B2	0.61mg
B3	1.2mg
B6	0.12mg
B12	0.00062mg
Folic Acid	–
C	0
✸D	11iu
E	0.7mg

Roquefort cheese is a semi-hard cheese which is made from the curds of ewes' milk. Special breadcrumbs which have developed a green mold are ground to a fine dust and mixed with the curds. The cheese is then stored in very cold caves to ripen. It may ripen in a few months, but a good Roquefort will be stored for at least a year.

Roquefort should have a gray rind; the cheese inside should be yellowish, very fatty and evenly veined in blue. If it is too white and chalky, it has not ripened completely.

Similar "bleu" mold-made cheeses are Gorgonzola, Danish Blue, and Stilton. Some of these blue cheeses are made of a mixture of goats', ewes' and cows' milk; Stilton is made of full-cream milk.

Other semi-hard cheeses are Munster, Brick, Port du Salut, Bel Paese, Fontana, Gammelost, Gouda and Jack.

Brick cheese, a semi-hard cheese made from cows' milk, has over twice the amount of calcium (730mg) and more phosphorus than Roquefort. It has less of the B vitamins, with no B1, 0.45mg of B2 and 0.1mg of B3. The difference in calcium may just reflect the different calcium content of cows' and ewes' milk.

Brick and Emmenthal cheese are both ripened by bacteria that produce a gas which is trapped in the curd – thus forming the holes.

CHEESE
CAMEMBERT
100g/3½oz

NUTRITIONAL CONTENT	
Joules	1255.8
Calories	299
✹Proteins	17.5g
Carbohydrates	1.8g
✹Cholesterol	105mg
✹Fat	26g plus
Sat. fats	15g
Unsat. fats	9g plus
Fiber	0

Minerals

Phosphorus	184mg
✹Calcium	105mg
Iron	0.5mg
Sodium	—
Potassium	111mg
Magnesium	—

Vitamins

✹A	800iu
B1	0.04mg
✹B2	0.75mg
✹B3	0.8mg
B6	0.22mg
✹B12	0.0013mg
Folic Acid	—
C	0
✹D	8iu
E	—

Camembert is a fermented cheese made of curds from whole full-cream milk. It is a soft cheese invented by Mme. Harel, a farmer's wife in the village of Camembert in 1790. Made mainly in winter, it is "aged" on wicker trays of oat straw. A good Camembert must have a yellowish orange crust without any black streaks. The cheese must be pale yellow, smooth, without holes and firm. Cheeses of a similar nature are Brie, Coulommiers, Livarot and Pont l'Eveque.

The particular flavor of a cheese may come about through the type of feed given to the cows, the type of milk used (cow, sheep or goat), the type of bacteria produced, the climate, the addition of different herbs, and other variables.

NUTRITIONAL CONTENT

Joules	361.2
Calories	86
✱ Proteins	17g
Carbohydrates	2.7g
Cholesterol	5.6mg
Fat	0.3g
Sat. fats	–
Unsat. fats	–
Fiber	0

Minerals

Phosphorus	175mg
Calcium	90mg
Iron	0.4mg
✱ Sodium	290mg
Potassium	72mg
Magnesium	–

Vitamins

A	10iu
B1	0.03mg
✱ B2	0.28mg
B3	0.1mg
B6	–
B12	–
Folic Acid	–
C	0
D	–
E	–

Cottage cheese is an unripened, fresh, soft curd cheese which must be refrigerated. The size of the curds does not affect the nutritional content of the cheese.

The addition of cream (creamed cottage cheese) enriches it enormously. It is no longer a low-fat and low-cholesterol cheese. Just 4 percent of cream will increase the cholesterol to 15mg, the calories to 106, and the fat content to 4.2g, of which only 1.3g will be unsaturated. Cream will also increase the calcium content substantially (94mg), lessening the phosphorus (152mg). The other minerals and most of the other vitamins will change slightly. The vitamin A content will be increased to 170iu. All creamed cottage cheeses will have a vitamin D content.

Similar cheese are farmers cheese, pot cheese, neufchatel, primost, ricotta, Gervaise and cream cheese.

CHEESE
CREAM (FULL-FAT SOFT)
100g/3½oz

NUTRITIONAL CONTENT	
Joules	1570.8
Calories	374
Proteins	8g
Carbohydrates	2.1g
✻Cholesterol	120mg
✻Fat	37.7g
Sat. fats	21g
Unsat. fats	13g
Fiber	0

Minerals
Phosphorus	95mg
Calcium	62mg
Iron	0.2mg
✻Sodium	250mg
Potassium	74mg
Magnesium	–

Vitamins
✻A	1540iu
B1	0.02mg
✻B2	0.24mg
B3	0.1
B6	0.005mg
B12	0.00022mg
Folic Acid	–
C	0
✻D	35iu
E	–

There are several ways of making **cream cheese**. Double cream can be added to milk before introducing the rennet, or it may be made from milk which has been completely skimmed. The cheese is worked with fresh cream after draining and put into molds to complete the drainage.

It is very rich in calories, fats, cholesterol and vitamin A, but contains only a little calcium.

Cream cheese must be refrigerated.

Cream cheese is a full-fat soft cheese, which does not have to be made from cream. In Great Britain, the name "Philadelphia cream cheese" had to be changed to "Philadelphia full-fat soft cheese" because it did not contain sufficient cream to justify the use of the name under the consumer protection laws.

NUTRITIONAL CONTENT

Joules	1554
Calories	370
✹ Proteins	27.5g
Carbohydrates	1.7g
✹ Cholesterol	98mg
✹ Fat	28g
Sat. fats	15g
Unsat. fats	10g
Fiber	0

Minerals

✹ Phosphorus	563mg
✹ Calcium	925mg
Iron	0.9mg
✹ Sodium	710mg
Potassium	104mg
Magnesium	–

Vitamins

✹ A	1140iu
B1	0.01mg
✹ B2	0.4mg
B3	0.1mg
B6	0.075mg
✹ B12	0.0018mg
Folic Acid	–
C	0
D	–
E	0.4mg

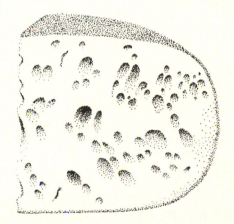

Swiss (Emmenthal) cheese originated in small mountain villages where it was usually made from whole fat milk, because of the difficulties involved in transporting more perishable dairy products. Nowadays it contains less milk fat.

It is a hard cheese, made in large round shapes with a straw-colored rind. The holes or "eyes" made by gas-producing bacteria are fairly large, but should not exceed the size of a quarter or ten-pence piece.

100g will contain 3.9mg zinc.

It is an excellent cooking cheese, and should be grated before use.

CHEESE
SWISS PASTEURIZED PROCESSED
100g/3½oz

NUTRITIONAL CONTENT

Joules	1491
Calories	355
✳ Proteins	26.4g
Carbohydrates	1.6g
✳ Cholesterol	85mg
✳ Fat	26.9g
Sat. fats	15g
Unsat. fats	10g
Fiber	0

Minerals

✳ Phosphorus	867mg
✳ Calcium	887mg
Iron	0.9mg
✳ Sodium	1167mg
Potassium	100mg
Magnesium	–

Vitamins

✳ A	1100iu
B1	0.01mg
✳ B2	0.4mg
B3	0.1mg
B6	0.043mg
✳ B12	0.0012mg
✳ Folic Acid	11mcg
C	0
✳ D	12iu
E	–

Pasteurized Swiss cheese is made from a mixture of new and old cheeses, emulsifiers and water. It has slightly less food value than natural Swiss cheese, but is still high in calories, proteins, calcium and vitamin A. It also contains 3.6mg of zinc.

Pasteurized processed Swiss cheese food may contain up to 44 percent water or milk. It has less food value than processed Swiss cheese, but still contains a large amount of proteins, calcium and vitamin A. It has 323 calories, 22g of protein, 5g of carbohydrates, 82mg of cholesterol and 25g of fat. There is 723mg of calcium, a large amount of salt, 1,552mg, and 3.5mg of zinc. It also has a fairly large amount of vitamin A (856iu).

NUTRITIONAL CONTENT

Joules	294
Calories	70
Proteins	1.3g
✹ Carbohydrates	17.4g
Cholesterol	0
Fat	0.3g
Sat. fats	–
Unsat. fats	–
✹ Fiber	0.4g

Minerals

Phosphorus	19mg
Calcium	22mg
Iron	0.4mg
Sodium	2mg
Potassium	191mg
Magnesium	–

Vitamins

✹ A	110iu
B1	0.05mg
B2	0.06mg
✹ B3	0.4mg
B6	0.032mg
B12	–
Folic Acid	–
✹ C	10mg
D	0
E	–

Sour cherries differ from sweet cherries in having less sugar. They also have less calories (58) and less carbohydrates (14.3g) but contain far more vitamin A (1000iu). In all other respects they are similar.

The use of heavy sugar syrup eliminates the difference in **canned cherries** (sweet 81 calories, sour 89 calories). The two kinds resemble each other in all ways except for their vitamin A content. Sour canned cherries have 650iu of vitamin A while sweet canned cherries have only 60iu. Canned cherries and fresh cherries differ very little in other respects.

Candied cherries are in fact candy. With an enormous calorie content (339) and high in carbohydrates (86.7g), they have very little fiber (0.5g) or protein (0.5g).

CHICKEN: fryer
FLESH AND SKIN (FRIED)
100g/3½oz

NUTRITIONAL CONTENT	
Joules	1050
Calories	250
✹Proteins	30.6g
Carbohydrates	2.8g
✹Cholesterol	86.4mg
✹Fat	11.8g
Sat. fats	3g
Unsat. fats	8g
Fiber	0

Minerals

✹Phosphorus	243mg
Calcium	12mg
Iron	1.8mg
Sodium	–
Potassium	–
Magnesium	–

Vitamins

A	170iu
B1	0.06mg
✹B2	0.36mg
✹B3	9.2mg
✹B6	0.683mg
✹B12	0.00045mg
✹Folic Acid	3.1mcg
C	0
D	0
E	0.3mg

Chickens are normally divided into the following categories for selling: a poussin is a small chicken weighing up to 1½lbs; a spring chicken weighs between 1½ and 3lbs; fryers are usually young chickens weighing between 2½ and 3½lbs and are fatter than the other two.

There are three ways of frying: deep fat frying which consists of total immersion of the chicken in fat at 375°F; pan frying; and sautéing (agitating and searing). Fried chicken will absorb some of the fat it is cooked in. To avoid high cholesterol and saturated fat it is advisable to fry with vegetable oils. The figures here refer to chicken fried in vegetable oil.

NUTRITIONAL CONTENT

Joules	1041.6
Calories	248
✹Proteins	27.1g
Carbohydrates	0
✹Cholesterol	86.4mg
✹Fat	14.7g
Sat. fats	–
Unsat. fats	–
Fiber	0

Minerals

✹ Phosphorus	239mg
Calcium	11mg
Iron	1.8mg
Sodium	–
Potassium	–
Magnesium	–

Vitamins

A	420iu
B1	0.08mg
B2	0.14mg
✹B3	8.2mg
✹B6	0.683mg
✹B12	0.00045mg
✹Folic Acid	3.1mcg
C	0
D	0
E	0.3mg

The best chickens for roasting are called roasters. They can be of either sex, are about 8 months old and weigh from 3½ to 5½ lbs. Capons — castrated male chickens — weighing from 6 to 8 lbs, are also excellent. Both roasters and capons have a layer of fat under their skin, which bastes the bird as it cooks.

A young and fresh chicken has a moist skin, soft legs and, most important of all, a pliable breast bone. If its breast bone is stiff or its skin hard, purplish, broken or bruised, the bird is past its prime.

Frozen chickens should not have any odd marks. Marks on the skin may indicate freezer burns from improper storage.

CHICKEN: hens and cocks

FLESH AND SKIN (STEWED)
100g/3½oz

NUTRITIONAL CONTENT	
Joules	1331.4
Calories	317
✹ Proteins	26.1g
Carbohydrates	0
✹ Cholesterol	86.4mg
✹ Fat	22.8g
Sat. fats	7g
Unsat. fats	14g
Fiber	0
Minerals	
Phosphorus	134mg
Calcium	11mg
Iron	1.5mg
Sodium	–
Potassium	–
Magnesium	–
Vitamins	
A	670iu
B1	0.04mg
B2	0.14mg
✹ B3	8.8mg
B6	–
B12	–
Folic Acid	–
C	0
D	0
E	–

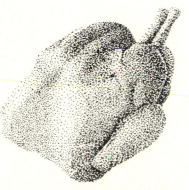

Fowl is a polite term for an old, tough hen aged 10 months or more.

Stag or cock is the name for male chickens too old and tough to roast. They should only be braised, boiled or stewed.

NUTRITIONAL CONTENT

Joules	4.2
Calories	1
Proteins	trace
Carbohydrates	trace
Cholesterol	0
Fat	trace
Sat. fats	–
Unsat. fats	–
Fiber	trace

Minerals
Phosphorus	4mg
Calcium	2mg
Iron	0.1mg
Sodium	1mg
Potassium	36mg
Magnesium	–

Vitamins
A	0
B1	0
B2	trace
B3	0.3mg
B6	trace
B12	–
Folic Acid	–
C	0
D	–
E	–

Instant coffee without milk or sugar added contains few nutrients. Instant coffee prepared with water and coffee powder has only 1 calorie, 4mg phosphorus, 2mg calcium and 36mg potassium, but it does have more sodium (1mg). It contains traces of protein, carbohydrates, fat, fiber, vitamin B2 and B1. It also has a slight amount of vitamin B3. An 8-oz cup of instant coffee made with a teaspoon of coffee will contain 35 to 45mg of caffeine.

111

COFFEE: percolated
MADE WITH 60g GROUND ROASTED BEANS
100ml/3½ fluid oz

NUTRITIONAL CONTENT	
Joules	12.6
Calories	3
Proteins	0.2g
Carbohydrates	0.3g
Cholesterol	0
Fat	trace
Sat. fats	–
Unsat. fats	–
Fiber	–
Minerals	
Phosphorus	1.5mg
Calcium	2.1mg
Iron	trace
Sodium	0.2mg
Potassium	66mg
Magnesium	5.5mg
Vitamins	
A	0
B1	0
B2	0.2mg
✱ B3	10mg
B6	–
B12	–
Folic Acid	–
C	0
D	–
E	–

Black coffee, whether instant or plain, never contains a large amount of nutrients.

The longer a coffee bean is roasted, the more vitamin B3 (niacin) it will contain. A dark roasted blend can contain more than three or four times the amount found in a "regular" roasted blend.

The longer the coffee is brewed, the stronger the brew will be, increasing the amount of some nutrients. If coffee is brewed for ten minutes, it will gain two more calories (total 5 calories) and will contain 104mg of potassium and 10.5mg of magnesium.

NUTRITIONAL CONTENT

Joules	218
Calories	52
Proteins	0.5g
✱ Carbohydrates	6g
Cholesterol	–
Fat	3g
Sat. fats	1g
Unsat. fats	1g
Fiber	–

Minerals

Phosphorus	–
Calcium	3mg
Iron	0.2mg
Sodium	35mg
Potassium	12mg
Magnesium	–

Vitamins

A	10iu
B1	0.01mg
B2	0.01mg
B3	0.1mg
B6	–
B12	–
Folic Acid	–
C	trace
D	–
E	–

Vanilla sandwich cookies have approx. the same energy nutrients, but more sodium (48mg), less potassium (4mg) and only slight traces of vitamins.

Shortbread has less calories (37), fat and carbohydrate (1.7g and 4.8g respectively), much less sodium (4mg) and potassium (5mg), and a small amount of vitamin A (101iu).

Chocolate wafers have 29 calories, less fat (1g), less carbohydrate (4.6g), less sodium (9mg) and the same amount of vitamins as a chocolate chip cookie.

Brownies with nuts have 97 calories, 1.3g protein, 6.2g fat, 10g carbohydrate, 8mg calcium, 0.4mg iron, 50mg sodium, 38mg potassium, 40iu vitamin A, 0.04mg vitamin B1, 0.03mg vitamin B2 and 0.1mg vitamin B3.

If you add chocolate icing you can end up with a calorific value of 119 calories.

Vanilla wafers have 18 calories, 0.2g protein, 0.6g fat, 3g carbohydrate, 2mg calcium, 10mg sodium, and very little potassium (3mg). Their vitamin content is 10iu vitamin A, with traces of the B vitamins.

113

CORN

KERNELS, OFF THE COB, BOILED AND DRAINED
100g/3½oz

Cooked **corn on the cob** has slightly more (8) calories and much more potassium (196mg).

All **canned corn** has a large amount of salt (236mg of sodium). Creamed, vacuum packed or in liquid, canned kernels of corn have similar nutritional content, and also contain approximately the same amount of nutrients as fresh kernels.

Dietary canned corn has practically no salt. It has less vitamin A (270iu).

Frozen corn when cooked is like fresh cooked corn.

Cornmeal and **cornflour** have a similar amount of calories (368), carbohydrates (76g) and fats (3g).

Enriched cornmeal has more iron (2.9g) and more B vitamins (0.44mg B1, 0.26mg B2, 3.5mg B3). **Self-raising cornmeal** will have more calcium. **Cooked cornmeal** which is not enriched has about 1/7 of the vitamins of enriched cornmeal. Cooked cornmeal of all types will have an 88 percent water content, 50 calories, 11g of carbohydrates, 1g of protein and practically no fat (0.2g).

A medium-sized corn muffin, weighing one ounce, made with enriched flour, will contain 90 calories, 2g protein, 2.7g fat, 14g carbohydrates, 30g calcium, 137mg sodium, 38.5g potassium, 86iu vitamin A, 0.6 B1, 0.08 B2, 0.4 B3. Corn bread has the same nutritional values as corn muffins.

For cornflakes, see *Breakfast cereal*, p.89.

NUTRITIONAL CONTENT

Joules	348.6
Calories	83
Proteins	3.2g
✱ Carbohydrates	18.8g
Cholesterol	0
Fat	1g
Sat. fats	—
Unsat. fats	—
✱ Fiber	0.7g

Minerals

Phosphorus	89mg
Calcium	3mg
Iron	0.6mg
Sodium	trace
Potassium	165mg
Magnesium	—

Vitamins

A	400iu
B1	0.11mg
B2	0.1mg
B3	1.3mg
B6	—
B12	—
Folic Acid	—
C	7mg
D	—
E	—

114

NUTRITIONAL CONTENT

Joules	390.6
Calories	93
✸ Proteins	17.3g
Carbohydrates	0.5g
✸ Cholesterol	62mg
Fat	1.9g
Sat. fats	—
Unsat. fats	—
Fiber	—

Minerals

Phosphorus	137mg
Calcium	43mg
Iron	0.8mg
Sodium	—
Potassium	—
Magnesium	34mg

Vitamins

A	trace
B1	0.16mg
B2	0.08mg
✸ B3	2.8mg
B6	0.35mg
✸ B12	0.5mcg
Folic Acid	trace
C	2mg
D	0
E	—

Canned crabs have a very large amount of salt (1000mg).

Deviled crab made with bread cubes, butter, parsley, eggs, lemon juice, catsup and crab has 188 calories, 11.4g protein, 9.4g fat, 13.3g carbohydrates, 45mg calcium and 192mg phosphorus, 1.2mg iron, 867mg sodium, 166mg potassium and very few vitamins.

Crab Imperial is made with butter, flour, milk, onion, green pepper, eggs, lemon juice and crab meat. It contains 147 calories, 14.6g protein, 7.6g fat, 3.9g carbohydrates, 60mg calcium, 166mg phosphorus, 9mg iron, 728mg sodium and 131mg potassium.

CREAM

LIGHT, TABLE
1 tablespoon/14g/½oz

NUTRITIONAL CONTENT	
Joules	123
Calories	29
Proteins	0.4g
✸ Carbohydrates	0.55g
✸ Cholesterol	10mg
✸ Fat	2.9g
Sat. fats	1.8g
Unsat. fats	0.9g
Fiber	0
Minerals	
✸ Phosphorus	12mg
✸ Calcium	14mg
Iron	0.01mg
Sodium	6mg
✸ Potassium	18mg
Magnesium	1mg
Vitamins	
✸ A	108iu
B1	0.005mg
B2	0.022mg
B3	0.009mg
B6	0.005mg
B12	0.033mg
Folic Acid	trace
C	0.11mg
✸ D	7iu
E	–

Cream taken from cows in the summer will be one third richer in vitamins A, D, and E than cream taken from cows in winter.

The thicker the cream, the higher will be the fat content, calories and vitamin A; the protein, mineral and vitamin B content will be lower.

Half and half: 1 tablespoon contain 20 calories, 1.72g fats, 0.44g proteins, 18mg calcium, 65iu vitamin A and 6mg cholesterol.

Light whipping cream: 1 tablespoon contains 44 calories, 4.64g fats, 0.32g proteins, 10mg calcium, 169iu vitamin A and 17mg cholesterol.

Heavy whipping cream: 1 tablespoon contains 52 calories, 5.55g fats, 0.31g proteins, 10mg calcium, 220iu vitamin A and 21mg cholesterol.

Cultured sour cream: 1 tablespoon contains 26 calories, 2.52g fats, 0.38g proteins, 14mg calcium, 95iu vitamin A, 5mg cholesterol and 1.57g of saturated fat.

Sour cream — half and half: 1 tablespoon contains 20 calories, 1.8g fats, 0.44g proteins, 16mg calcium, 68iu vitamin A and 6mg cholesterol and 1.12g saturated fat.

Imitation sour cream: 1 tablespoon has 30 calories, 3g fats, 0.3g proteins, 0.5mg calcium, no vitamin A and cholesterol, but almost all saturated fats.

The low caloric, carbohydrate and fat content has prompted cooking experts to advise people on weight-reduction diets to use real sour cream in their cooking rather than cream.

116

NUTRITIONAL CONTENT	
Joules	134.4
Calories	32
Proteins	2.6g
Carbohydrates	5.5g
Cholesterol	0
Fat	0.7g
Sat. fats	–
Unsat. fats	–
✺Fiber	1.1g
Minerals	
Phosphorus	76mg
Calcium	81mg
Iron	1.3mg
Sodium	14mg
✺Potassium	606mg
Magnesium	–
Vitamins	
✺A	9300iu
B1	0.08mg
✺B2	0.26mg
B3	1mg
B6	0.247mg
B12	0
Folic Acid	–
✺C	69mg
D	–
E	0.7mg

Cress is a very underrated vegetable. It has very few of the "energy nutrients," but is extremely rich in minerals and vitamins.

When cress is boiled, it still retains a large amount of calcium (61mg), phosphorus (48mg), potassium (353mg) and 7700iu of vitamin A. It keeps 0.6mg of vitamin B1, 0.16mg of B2, 0.8mg of B3 and 34mg of vitamin C.

Watercress has 19 calories (79.8j), 2.2g of protein, 0.7g of fiber. It has 152mg of calcium, 54mg of phosphorus, 1.7mg of iron, 52mg of sodium, and 282mg of potassium. It has a large amount of vitamin A (4900iu), 0.08mg of B1, 0.16mg of B2, 0.9mg of B3 and 79mg of vitamin C. It contains 50mg of folic acid.

CUCUMBER
RAW, UNPARED
100g/3½oz

NUTRITIONAL CONTENT	
Joules	63
Calories	15
Proteins	0.9g
Carbohydrates	3.4g
Cholesterol	0
Fat	0.1g
Sat. fats	–
Unsat. fats	–
✹ Fiber	0.6g
Minerals	
Phosphorus	27mg
Calcium	25mg
Iron	1.1mg
Sodium	6mg
Potassium	160mg
Magnesium	11mg
Vitamins	
A	250mg
B1	0.03mg
B2	0.04mg
B3	0.2mg
B6	0.042mg
B12	0
✹ Folic Acid	6.7mcg
✹ C	11mg
D	0
E	0.1mg

Cucumbers are 95 percent water. When peeled, they lose a minute amount of energy-producing nutrients and minerals, and all their vitamin A.

NUTRITIONAL CONTENT	
Joules	1150.8
Calories	274
Proteins	2.2g
✳Carbohydrates	72.9g
Cholesterol	0
Fat	0.5g
Sat. fats	—
Unsat. fats	—
✳Fiber	2.3g

Minerals

Phosphorus	63mg
Calcium	59mg
Iron	3mg
Sodium	1mg
✳Potassium	648mg
Magnesium	58mg

Vitamins

A	50iu
B1	0.09mg
B2	0.1mg
✳B3	2.2mg
B6	0.153mg
B12	0
✳Folic Acid	24.9mcg
C	0
D	0
E	—

For the last 4,000 years, **dates** have been food for the wandering tribes of North Africa and Arabia. They grow wild in the valley of the Tigris.

They are now commercially produced in Tunisia, Algeria and western Africa. In the United States they are commercially produced in Arizona and South Carolina.

They are highly nutritious, with a large calorie, carbohydrate, potassium and folic acid content.

DRINKS: alcoholic

BEER, 4.5% ALCOHOL (BY VOLUME)
100ml/3½fluid oz

Beer can be brewed from almost any cereal, but is usually made from barley flavored with hops. Sometimes corn or rice is added for flavoring.

Beer has a high vitamin B content.

Unfermented carbohydrates help to give beer body and a distinctive taste. The special types of water used may also add to the taste. The head is formed by the carbon dioxide contained in the beer.

Pale ale is made from malt which has just been dried.

Dark beer comes from highly roasted malt colored by adding burnt sugar or caramel.

American-style beer (lager) comes from bottom fermentation.

Porter, stout ale and English beer come from top fermentation.

Beer was known to the ancient Egyptians. 5,000 years ago they had licensing regulations to prevent the local population from overindulging in drink at the beer shops.

One learned doctor says man's desire for fermented drink is what separates him from the animals who are happy with water.

NUTRITIONAL CONTENT	
Joules	180.6
Calories	42
Proteins	0.3g
Carbohydrates	3.8g
Cholesterol	0
Fat	0
Sat. fats	–
Unsat. fats	–
Fiber	0
Minerals	
Phosphorus	30mg
Calcium	5mg
Iron	trace
Sodium	7mg
Potassium	25mg
Magnesium	–
Vitamins	
A	0
B1	trace
B2	0.03mg
✴ B3	0.6mg
B6	0.06mg
B12	0
Folic Acid	–
C	0
D	–
E	–

NUTRITIONAL CONTENT

Joules	970.2
Calories	231
Proteins	0
Carbohydrates	trace
Cholesterol	0
Fat	0
Sat. fats	–
Unsat. fats	–
Fiber	0

Minerals

Phosphorus	0
Calcium	0
Iron	0
Sodium	1mg
Potassium	2mg
Magnesium	0

Vitamins

A	0
B1	0
B2	0
B3	0
B6	0
B12	0
Folic Acid	0
C	0
D	0
E	0

Rum is made from fermented and distilled sugar-cane products.

Whiskey is distilled from a fermented mash of grains; rye, barley, oats, wheat or corn. **Scotch Whisky** is made from fermented barley mixtures, using peat to cure the malt. The rich brown color comes from the casks in which it is distilled.

Gin is liquor distilled from fermented cereals and flavored with juniper berries. **Sloe gin** is flavored with sloes instead of juniper.

The higher the proof of these spirits i.e., percentage of alcohol, the more calories they have:

86 percent proof – 249 calories
90 percent proof – 263 calories
94 percent proof – 275 calories
100 percent proof – 295 calories

The other nutrients do not increase with the caloric values but remain constant.

DRINKS: alcoholic

TABLE WINES, 12.2% ALCOHOL (BY VOLUME)
100g/100ml/3½fluid oz

Wines are made by the fermentation of grape juice, or the juices of berries or flowers. This section is concerned only with grape wines.

Wines are distinguished by color, aroma, flavor and alcoholic content. They can be still (most table wine), fortified (brandies, vermouths, sherries) or sparkling (champagne).

Different wines are made through the use of different grapes and through variation in the length of fermentation time.

When making red wine the whole grape, including the juice, pips or seeds and skin, is left to ferment.

When making rosé wine the skin and pips are removed after fermentation has begun.

For white wine, it is customary to use only the juice of the grapes.

If the grape juice is allowed to ferment completely, it will produce a dry wine, but if the fermentation is not complete when the wine is bottled, there will be sugar left and the wine will be a sweet wine.

Sweet wine frequently has a higher alcoholic content than dry wine and is much more fattening. It can have twice the carbohydrates and up to 70 percent more calories.

NUTRITIONAL CONTENT	
Joules	357
Calories	85
Proteins	0.1g
Carbohydrates	4.2g
Cholesterol	0
Fat	0
Sat. fats	–
Unsat. fats	–
Fiber	0
Minerals	
Phosphorus	10mg
Calcium	9mg
Iron	0.4mg
Sodium	5mg
Potassium	92mg
Magnesium	6–13mg
Vitamins	
A	0
B1	trace
B2	0.01mg
B3	0.1mg
B6	0.04mg
B12	0
Folic Acid	–
C	0
D	0
E	–

NUTRITIONAL CONTENT

Joules	163.8
Calories	39
Proteins	0
Carbohydrates	10g
Cholesterol	0
Fat	0
Sat. fats	0
Unsat. fats	0
Fiber	0

Minerals

Phosphorus	0
Calcium	0
Iron	0
Sodium	0
Potassium	0
Magnesium	0

Vitamins

A	0
B1	0
B2	0
B3	0
B6	0
B12	0
Folic Acid	0
C	0
D	0
E	0

Carbonated (fizzy) drinks are made by dissolving carbon dioxide in water.

Club soda is just carbonated water and has no calories, no carbohydrates and no other nutrients.

Other carbonated drinks will be made in the same way, but the water will contain additives.

They usually only contain calories, carbohydrates and no other nutrients.

Beverages	Calories	Carbohydrates
Quinine ("tonic") water	31	8g
Club soda (unsweetened)	0	0
Cola type	39	10g
Cream soda	43	11g
Fruit-flavored soda	46	12g
Tom Collins mixer	46	12g
Ginger ale (all types)	31	8g
Root beer	41	10.5g
Special dietary drinks with artificial sweetener	0	0

There is no other food value to be found in these drinks.

DUCK
ROAST, FLESH ONLY
100g/3½oz

NUTRITIONAL CONTENT	
Joules	1314.6
Calories	313
✴ Proteins	22.8g
Carbohydrates	0
✴ Cholesterol	87mg
✴ Fat	23.6g
Sat. fats	–
Unsat. fats	–
Fiber	–
Minerals	
✴ Phosphorus	231mg
Calcium	19mg
✴ Iron	5.8mg
✴ Sodium	195mg
✴ Potassium	319mg
Magnesium	23.9mg
Vitamins	
A	–
B1	–
B2	–
B3	–
B6	–
B12	–
Folic Acid	–
C	–
D	–
E	–

Domestic ducks have large frames and a great deal of fat. Age and tenderness can be determined by the flexibility of the underbill. Normally an uncooked duck weighs between 5 and 6lbs, while a duckling weighs 3-4½lbs.

To determine how large a duck you will need to serve, allow 1½lbs of raw duck per serving; the bulk added by the fat will be lost in the cooking, much of it absorbed by the meat. The cooked meat will have almost twice as many calories and 3 times the fat content of the raw duck.

The famous **Rouen duck** of France has a unique taste and dark red-colored flesh caused by its being smothered, rather than slaughtered or bled. It must be cooked the same day it is killed to avoid possible food poisoning. They are seldom marketed in the United States.

The flesh of a wild duck will have less calories, fat and more protein than a farmyard duck.

124

EGGPLANT (AUBERGINE)
BOILED AND DRAINED
100g/3½oz

NUTRITIONAL CONTENT

Joules	79.8
Calories	19
Proteins	1g
Carbohydrates	4.1g
Cholesterol	–
Fat	0.2g
Sat. fats	–
Unsat. fats	–
Fiber	0.9g

Minerals

Phosphorus	21mg
Calcium	11mg
Iron	0.6mg
Sodium	1mg
Potassium	150mg
Magnesium	–

Vitamins

A	10iu
B1	0.05mg
B2	0.04mg
✹B3	0.5mg
B6	0.081mg
B12	0
Folic Acid	–
C	3mg
D	–
E	–

There are many varieties of edible eggplant (aubergine): the long purple, the round purple, the giant New York, the round Chinese, and the Barbentane. No matter which variety is cooked, it should always be covered with salt for 30 minutes before cooking to draw out the excess water content.

Eggplant absorbs large amounts of fat when it is cooked which increases its calories and fat content.

A favorite story is told about a dish called Aubergine "Imam Baaldi" (Eggplant "Fainting Priest"). An *imam* adored a dish his fiancée prepared so much that he asked for her dowry to be paid in the oil in which it was cooked. Huge jars filled with oil were stored in every room in the house. For the first two nights of their marriage she served him his favorite dish. On the third night, she gave him something else. Disappointed, he asked her why she had not prepared the special dish. "Alas," said the wife, "the first two nights have exhausted our supply of oil," at which the greedy *imam* fainted. The dish called for eggplant halves stuffed with fried eggplant, tomatoes, currants and onions and baked for 3 hours in a casserole in which the stuffed eggplants are completely covered with oil.

125

EGGS

RAW, FRESH AND FROZEN

2 large/100g/3½oz

All fresh chicken **eggs** of the same size and age have the same food values. The value of the nutrients found in eggs is the same whether the eggs are white shelled, brown shelled, have light yolks or dark yolks.

If the shells are shiny, the eggs are past their prine. Eggs that float in cold water are not usable. A fresh egg should have a yolk that domes up and a thick and translucent white that does not spread over the plate.

All the cholesterol and fat in eggs will be found in the yolk. Half the folic acid present in raw eggs will be lost in cooking. The longer eggs are stored, the less vitamin B12 they will contain.

Hard boiled eggs and raw eggs have the same food values, except for the folic acid content.

Omelets and scrambled eggs cooked in butter have slightly more calories (173), 2.4g carbohydrates and 12.9g fat. They have slightly less protein (11.2g), 189mg phosphorus and 1.7mg iron. They have 257mg sodium, 80mg calcium and also contain slightly less vitamins.

Two fried eggs cooked in butter have more calories (216), 13.8g protein, 17g fat, 338g sodium, and 1420 iu of vitamin A. The other nutrients also increase slightly.

126

NUTRITIONAL CONTENT

Joules	684.6
Calories	163
✳Proteins	12.9g
Carbohydrates	0.9g
✳Cholesterol	550mg
✳Fat	11.5g
Sat. fats	4g
Unsat. fats	6g
Fiber	0

Minerals

✳Phosphorus	205mg
Calcium	54mg
✳Iron	2.3mg
Sodium	122mg
Potassium	129mg
Magnesium	11mg

Vitamins

✳A	1180 iu
B1	0.11mg
✳B2	0.3mg
B3	0.1mg
B6	0.06mg
✳B12	0.8mcg
✳Folic Acid	32mcg
C	0
✳D	70 iu
✳E	2mg

NUTRITIONAL CONTENT

Joules	84
Calories	20
Proteins	1.7g
Carbohydrates	4.1g
Cholesterol	0
Fat	0.1g
Sat. fats	–
Unsat. fats	–
✷ Fiber	0.9g

Minerals

Phosphorus	54mg
Calcium	81mg
Iron	1.7mg
Sodium	14mg
✷ Potassium	294mg
Magnesium	10mg

Vitamins

✷ A	3300 iu
B1	0.07mg
B2	0.14mg
B3	0.5mg
B6	0.02mg
B12	0
✷ Folic Acid	63.7mcg
✷ C	10mg
D	0
✷ E	2mg

There are two types of endive: the **curly-leaved crisp type** similar to lettuce, normally used for salads; and the **Batavian broad-leaved endive,** normally used in cooking.

The Batavian endive is kept white by covering its leaves while it is growing. This excludes light and prevents the development of the bitter taste.

There is continual confusion over names. In England, endive is what the Americans call chicory, and chicory that which the Americans call endive. They are just different varieties of the same plant.

FARINA
COOKED REGULAR
100g/3½oz

NUTRITIONAL CONTENT	
Joules	176.4
Calories	42
Proteins	1.3g
✱ Carbohydrates	8.7g
Cholesterol	0
Fat	0.1g
Sat. fats	–
Unsat. fats	–
Fiber	trace
Minerals	
Phosphorus	12mg
Calcium	4mg
Iron	0.3mg
✱ Sodium	144mg
Potassium	9mg
Magnesium	3mg
Vitamins	
A	0
B1	0.04mg
B2	0.03mg
B3	0.4mg
B6	–
B12	–
Folic Acid	–
C	0
D	–
E	–

Any product which is "enriched" or has additives will have arbitrary amounts of iron, B vitamins and frequently calcium. Different brands may have different amounts.

Instant cooked Farina has slightly more calories (55), a little more protein (1.7mg), 11.4mg of carbohydrates, more calcium (77mg) and sodium (188mg). The iron and B vitamins also increase.

NUTRITIONAL CONTENT	
Joules	550.2
Calories	131
Proteins	trace
Carbohydrates	0
Cholesterol	13mg
✸Fat	14g
Sat. fats	5.4g
Unsat. fats	8g
Fiber	0
Minerals	
Phosphorus	0.5mg
Calcium	0.1mg
Iron	0.01mg
Sodium	0.3mg
Potassium	0.1mg
Magnesium	0.2mg
Vitamins	
A	–
B1	–
B2	–
B3	–
B6	–
B12	–
Folic Acid	–
C	–
D	–
E	–

Suet (raw beef kidney fat), **beef drippings** and other cooking fats all have the same calories, cholesterol and fat content.

Suet has more mineral content, though this is still low. It has 6mg sodium, 4mg potassium and small amounts of iron (0.11mg), calcium (1.7mg) and magnesium (0.3mg).

Drippings have even less nutrients.

Compound kitchen cooking fats probably have faint traces of minerals.

FATS AND OILS
VEGETABLE COOKING FATS AND OILS
1 tablespoon/14.3g/½oz

NUTRITIONAL CONTENT	
Joules	530.4
Calories	126.3
Proteins	0
Carbohydrates	0
Cholesterol	0
✱ Fat	14.3g
Sat. fats	3.3g
Unsat. fats	10.3g
Fiber	0
Minerals	
Phosphorus	0
Calcium	0
Iron	0
Sodium	0
Potassium	0
Magnesium	0
Vitamins	
A	0
B1	0
B2	0
B3	0
B6	0
B12	0
Folic Acid	0
C	0
D	0
E	0

All **oils** have saturated and unsaturated fatty acids. Saturated fatty acids tend to raise the amount of cholesterol in the blood. Monosaturated fatty acids are neutral. They contain nothing harmful (like cholesterol) nor do they have any beneficial action. **Peanut and olive oil** contain large amounts of such acids.

Polyunsaturated fatty acids tend to help the body get rid of newly formed cholesterol, keep the cholesterol in the blood down, and reduce cholesterol deposits in the arterial walls. **Safflower, soybean, corn, cottonseed and sesame seed oils** have high concentration of such acids.

A **salad dressing** made with one tablespoonful of oil (63 calories) and one teaspoon of lemon juice (0.7 calories) has 63.7 calories. The lemon juice contains 5mg vitamin C, 14mg potassium and traces of other minerals and vitamins, and the made-up salad dressing contains the same.

A salad dressing made with one tablespoonful of oil and one teaspoonful of vinegar (0.3 calories) contains 63.3 calories and 14mg potassium from the vinegar.

Different oils have different amounts of vitamin E.

Refined corn oil	87mg
Refined olive oil	4.6mg
Refined peanut oil	21.2-21.7mg
Refined safflower oil	30.6mg
Refined soybean oil	60-72mg

See *Fats*, p. 129

NUTRITIONAL CONTENT

Joules	117.6
Calories	28
Proteins	2.8g
Carbohydrates	5.1g
Cholesterol	0
Fat	0.4g
Sat. fats	–
Unsat. fats	–
✹Fiber	0.5g

Minerals

Phosphorus	51mg
✹Calcium	100mg
✹Iron	2.7mg
Sodium	0
✹Potassium	397mg
Magnesium	–

Vitamins

✹A	3500 iu
B1	–
B2	–
B3	–
B6	–
B12	–
Folic Acid	–
✹C	31mg
D	–
E	–

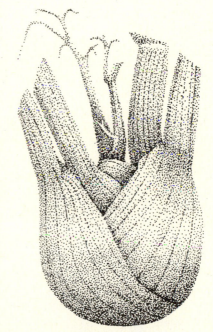

Fennel is an aromatic plant which has a slight licorice taste. The edible part of the plant is the base, which can be eaten raw or cooked.

The feathery leaves can be used for flavoring.

It sometimes has a faintly laxative effect.

FIGS
RAW
100g/3½oz

Candied figs have 299 calories, 74g carbohydrates and 1.6g fiber.

Dried figs have 274 calories, 69g carbohydrates, a large amount of potassium (640mg), 77mg calcium, 3mg iron and some vitamins.

Canned figs in heavy syrup (with each fig containing as much liquid as a fresh fig) have 84 calories, 22mg carbohydrates, almost no protein or fats, and less minerals and vitamins than fresh figs.

NUTRITIONAL CONTENT

Joules	533.4
Calories	127
✸ Proteins	19.5g
Carbohydrates	0
✸ Cholesterol	70mg
Fat	5.1g
Sat. fats	–
Unsat. fats	–
Fiber	0

Minerals

Phosphorus	220mg
✸ Calcium	46.9mg
Iron	0.7mg
Sodium	75mg
✸ Potassium	326mg
✸ Magnesium	26.9mg

Vitamins

A	–
B1	–
B2	–
B3	–
B6	–
B12	–
Folic Acid	–
C	–
D	–
E	–

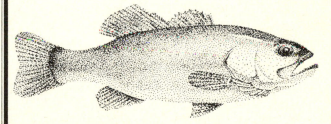

Oven-fried striped bass, dipped in milk and covered with bread crumbs, butter and salt, has 196 calories, 21.5g protein, 8.5g fat and 6.7g carbohydrates.

Black sea bass, stuffed and baked with bacon, butter, onion, celery and bread crumbs, has 259 calories, 16.2g protein, 15.8g fat and 11.4g carbohydrates.

FISH: COD
BROILED
100g/3½oz

NUTRITIONAL CONTENT	
Joules	714
Calories	170
✹ Proteins	28.5g
Carbohydrates	0
✹ Cholesterol	70mg
✹ Fat	5.3g
Sat. fats	–
Unsat. fats	–
Fiber	0
Minerals	
✹ Phosphorus	274mg
Calcium	31mg
Iron	1mg
Sodium	110rng
✹ Potassium	407mg
Magnesium	28mg
Vitamins	
A	180 iu
B1	0.08mg
B2	0.11mg
✹ B3	3mg
B6	–
B12	–
Folic Acid	
C	0
D	–
E	0

Canned cod has less calories (85), less proteins (19.2g) and less fat (0.3g) than fresh cod.

Haddock, a member of the cod family, is remarkably similar in nutrients. When haddock is fried, it doubles its calorie content (165), gains carbohydrates (5.8g) and fat (6.4g). There is an increase in the mineral content: 247mg phosphorus, 40mg calcium, 1.2mg iron, 177mg sodium and 348mg potassium. It can be assumed that fried cod will have the same increased food values.

Finnan haddies (smoked haddock) has 103 calories and 23.2g of protein.

Raw cod's roe (haddock's roe) has 130 calories, 24.4g protein, 2.3g fat, 1.5g carbohydrates, a little iron (0.6mg) and some B vitamins (0.10mg B1, 0.76mg B2, 1.4mg B3, also 0.165mg of B6 and 0.01mg of B12). There is very little vitamin C.

Cooked, baked or broiled cod's roe has a few less calories (126), less protein (22g), a little more fat (2.8g), and 1.9g of carbohydrates. It has 13mg of calcium, 402mg of phosphorus, 2.3mg of iron, 73mg of sodium and 132mg of potassium.

Canned cod's roe has 118 calories, 21.5g protein, 2.8g fat and 0.3g carbohydrates. It has 15mg calcium, 346mg phosphorus and 1.2mg iron. It contains 0.14mg vitamin B6 and 0.015mg vitamin B12.

Cod liver oil has 75,800 iu of vitamin A and 8,700 iu of vitamin D.

NUTRITIONAL CONTENT

Joules	1386
Calories	330
✳ Proteins	18.6g
Carbohydrates	0
Cholesterol	–
✳ Fat	27.8g
Sat. fats	6g
Unsat. fats	10g
Fiber	–

Minerals

Phosphorus	–
Calcium	–
Iron	–
Sodium	–
Potassium	–
Magnesium	–

Vitamins

A	–
B1	–
B2	–
B3	–
B6	–
B12	–
Folic Acid	–
C	–
D	–
E	–

Smoking is one way to preserve fish. It dries the fish out and in doing so rids the fish of the bacteria that would cause it to decay quickly.

Nowadays fish is usually smoked to give it a special flavor. Wood is used for the smoking; hardwood smoke leaves the best flavor.

There are five hundred species of eel. Sixteen of the species live in fresh water. They take one trip to the sea, to spawn, after which they die. The elevers (young eels) must swim back to the fresh water from the sea.

European and **American freshwater eels** are alike nutritionally.

Eel is a fatty fish, and slightly difficult to digest.

FISH: FLOUNDER

BAKED

100g/3½oz

NUTRITIONAL CONTENT	
Joules	848.4
Calories	202
✳Proteins	30g
Carbohydrates	0
Cholesterol	70mg
Fat	8.2g
Sat. fats	–
Unsat. fats	–
Fiber	0
Minerals	
✳Phosphorus	344mg
Calcium	23mg
Iron	1.4mg
✳Sodium	237mg
✳Potassium	587mg
Magnesium	–
Vitamins	
A	0
B1	0.07mg
B2	0.08mg
✳B3	2.5mg
B6	0.17mg
✳B12	0.0012mg
Folic Acid	–
C	2mg
D	–
E	–

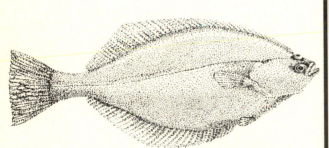

Steamed flounder has 95 calories, 19.4g protein, and 1.7g fat. It has 30.9mg calcium, 166mg phosphorus, 0.7mg iron.

Fried flounder, covered with batter and bread crumbs and fried in vegetable oil, has 214 calories, 17g protein, 12.9g fat, 6.5g carbohydrates and a large mineral content.

NUTRITIONAL CONTENT	
Joules	718.2
Calories	171
✹Proteins	25.2g
Carbohydrates	0
Cholesterol	73mg
Fat	7g
Sat. fats	–
Unsat. fats	–
Fiber	0
Minerals	
Phosphorus	248mg
Calcium	16mg
Iron	0.8mg
Sodium	134mg
✹Potassium	525mg
Magnesium	17.6mg
Vitamins	
A	680 iu
B1	0.05mg
B2	0.07mg
✹B3	8.3mg
B6	–
B12	–
Folic Acid	–
C	–
D	–
E	–

Halibut is a "fatty" fish.

Steamed halibut has 130 calories, a little less protein (22.7g) and less fat (4g). The vitamin and mineral content is similar.

Smoked halibut contains 224 calories, 20.8g protein and 15g fat.

FISH: HERRING

PICKLED, BISMARK TYPE

100g/3½oz

Prehistoric man ate herring: fossils of herring bones have been found in caves in Denmark.

Canned tomato herrings (herrings in tomato sauce) contain 176 calories, 15.8g protein, and 10.5g fat.

Canned herrings have 208 calories, 19.9g protein and 13.6g fat. They have a calcium content of 147mg, 297mg phosphorus and 1.8mg iron.

Salted herrings or herrings in brine have 218 calories, 19g protein and 15.2g fat. There will naturally be a large salt content.

Smoked herrings:

Bloaters have 196 calories, 19.6g protein and 12.4g fat.

Hard herrings have 300 calories, 36.9g protein and 15.8g fat. They also contain 6,231mg sodium and 157mg of potassium.

Kippers have 211 calories, 22.2g protein and 12.9g fat. They contain 66mg calcium, 254mg phosphorus and 1.4mg iron.

Herring roe has the same value as Cod's roe: see page 134.

NUTRITIONAL CONTENT	
Joules	936.6
Calories	223
✹ Proteins	20.4g
✹ Carbohydrates	0
Cholesterol	70mg
✹ Fat	15.1g
Sat. fats	2g
Unsat. fats	2g +
Fiber	0
Minerals	
✹ Phosphorus	272mg
✹ Calcium	101mg
Iron	1.5mg
Sodium	130mg
✹ Potassium	317mg
Magnesium	31.7mg
Vitamins	
A	150 iu
B1	0.03mg
✹ B2	0.3mg
✹ B3	3.5mg
✹ B6	0.45mg
✹ B12	10mcg
Folic Acid	–
C	trace
✹ D	900 iu
E	–

NUTRITIONAL CONTENT

Joules	785.4
Calories	187
✸ Proteins	20g
Carbohydrates	0
✸ Cholesterol	70mg
✸ Fat	11.3g
Sat. fats	–
Unsat. fats	–
Fiber	0

Minerals

✸ Phosphorus	280mg
Calcium	28.4mg
Iron	1.2mg
Sodium	153mg
✸ Potassium	418mg
Magnesium	34.8mg

Vitamins

A	430 iu
B1	0.15mg
✸ B2	0.27mg
✸ B3	7.6mg
B6	–
B12	–
Folic Acid	–
C	0
D	–
E	–

Cooked mackerel, broiled with butter or margarine, have more calories (236), more protein (21.8g), more fat (15.8g) and a vitamin content similar to that of raw mackerel.

Canned mackerel is similar to fried mackerel in its energy nutrients but has a little more iron (2.1mg) and a little less vitamin B1 (0.06mg).

Smoked mackerel has 219 calories, 23.8g protein and 13g fat.

Salted mackerel has 305 calories, 18.5g protein, 25g fat and a very high sodium and salt content.

FISH: SALMON

FRESH, BROILED OR BAKED
100g/3½oz

There are many types of salmon: Atlantic, Pacific, Chinook (King), Chum, Coho, Pink and Sockeye. They have different caloric values ranging from canned pink (141 calories) to canned King (210 calories). They have slightly different mineral contents as well.

Canned red salmon (Sockeye) has 171 calories, 20.3g protein, 9.3g fat, 259mg calcium, 344mg phosphorus, 1.2mg iron, 522mg sodium, 230 iu vitamin A, 0.04mg B2, 0.16mg B2, 7.3mg B3. (The calcium figure is misleading because it takes account of the calcium in the bones.)

In **canned red salmon without added salt** the values are the same, but the salt content is reduced by 48mg and the potassium increased to 391mg.

Canned pink salmon has 141 calories, 20.5g protein, 5.9g fat, 387mg sodium, 361mg potassium, and very little vitamin A.

Smoked salmon has 176 calories, 21.6g protein and 9.3g fat.

Raw salmon roe has 207 calories, 25.2g protein, 10.4g fat and 1.4g carbohydrates. There are B vitamins (0.38mg B1, 0.72mg B2 and 2.3mg B3) and a little vitamin C (18mg).

NUTRITIONAL CONTENT	
Joules	764.4
Calories	182
✸ Proteins	27g
Carbohydrates	0
✸ Cholesterol	70mg
Fat	7.4g
Sat. fats	–
Unsat. fats	–
Fiber	0
Minerals	
✸ Phosphorus	302mg
Calcium	28.9mg
Iron	0.8mg
Sodium	107mg
✸ Potassium	333mg
Magnesium	28.7mg
Vitamins	
A	160 iu
B1	0.16mg
B2	0.06mg
✸ B3	9.8mg
B6	0.3mg
✸ B12	2mcg
Folic Acid	5mcg
C	0
✸ D	500 iu
E	–

NUTRITIONAL CONTENT

Joules	1579.2
Calories	376.8
✷ Proteins	26.2g
Carbohydrates	0
✷ Cholesterol	169mg
✷ Fat	29.1g
Sat. fats	–
Unsat. fats	–
Fiber	0

Minerals

✷ Phosphorus	878.1mg
✷ Calcium	525.6mg
✷ Iron	5.1mg
✷ Sodium	1009mg
✷ Potassium	556.7mg
✷ Magnesium	53.01mg

Vitamins

A	128.57 iu
B1	trace
✷ B2	0.26mg
✷ B3	7.17mg
B6	0.2mg
✷ B12	12.9mcg
✷ Folic Acid	2.57mcg
C	trace
✷ D	385 iu
E	–

Each sardine in oil has approx. 75 calories. 100g of sardines canned in brine or mustard sauce have 196 calories, 18.8g protein, 12g fat and 1.7g carbohydrate. They have 303mg calcium, 354mg phosphorus, 5.2mg iron, 760mg sodium and 260mg potassium.

Sardines canned in tomato sauce contain approx. the same amount of calories, protein and carbohydrates as the fish canned in brine (per 100g) but they have less salt (400mg sodium), less iron (4.1mg), more potassium (320mg), more calcium (449mg) and more phosphorus (478mg). There is a small vitamin A and B content and 5.3mg vitamin B3.

FISH: SWORDFISH

BROILED, PREPARED WITH BUTTER OR MARGARINE

100g/3½oz

NUTRITIONAL CONTENT

Joules	730.8
Calories	174
✳ Proteins	28g
Carbohydrates	0
✳ Cholesterol	72mg
Fat	6g
Sat. fats	–
Unsat. fats	–
Fiber	0

Minerals

✳ Phosphorus	275mg
Calcium	27mg
Iron	1.3mg
Sodium	–
Potassium	–
Magnesium	–

Vitamins

✳ A	2050 iu
B1	0.04mg
B2	0.05mg
✳ B3	10.9mg
B6	–
B12	–
Folic Acid	–
C	0
D	–
E	–

Swordfish is low in fat and high in protein, vitamins, copper and iodine. Its bones are rich in calcium and phosphorus.

Swordfish baked or **broiled** without butter or margarine would have approximately the same amount of nutrients found in canned swordfish.

Canned swordfish has less calories (102), less protein (18g) and less fat (3g). It also has less vitamin A (1,580 iu) but slightly more vitamin B3 (11.4mg).

142

NUTRITIONAL CONTENT

Joules	558.6
Calories	133
✸Proteins	22.3g
Carbohydrates	0
✸Cholesterol	70mg
Fat	4.5g
Sat. fats	–
Unsat. fats	–
Fiber	0

Minerals

✸Phosphorus	270mg
Calcium	35.8mg
Iron	1mg
Sodium	88mg
✸Potassium	374mg
Magnesium	30.9mg

Vitamins

A	trace
B1	0.08mg
B2	0.06mg
✸B3	3mg
B6	–
B12	–
Folic Acid	–
C	trace
D	–
E	–

Canned rainbow trout has 209 calories, 20.6g protein, 13.4g fat and some B vitamins

FISH: TUNA

RAW

100g/3½oz

NUTRITIONAL CONTENT

Joules	609
Calories	145
✷ Proteins	25.2g
Carbohydrates	0
✷ Cholesterol	70mg
Fat	4.1g
Sat. fats	–
Unsat. fats	–
Fiber	0

Minerals

Phosphorus	–
Calcium	–
Iron	1.3mg
Sodium	–
Potassium	–
Magnesium	–

Vitamins

A	–
B1	–
B2	–
B3	–
✷ B6	0.9mg
✷ B12	0.003mg
Folic Acid	–
C	–
D	–
E	–

Tuna canned in oil and then drained has 197 calories, 28.8g protein, 8.2g fat, 8mg calcium, 0.234mg phosphorus and 1.9mg iron. It has 80 iu vitamin A, 0.5mg B1, 0.12mg B2 and 11.9mg B3.

A typical **Tuna salad** containing canned tuna, celery, mayonnaise, pickle, onion and egg has 170 calories, 14.6g protein, 10.5g fat, 3.5g carbohydrates, 20mg calcium, 142mg phosphorus, 1.3mg iron, and 290 iu vitamin A. It will have slightly less vitamin B3.

NUTRITIONAL CONTENT

Joules	739.2
Calories	176
✳ Proteins	16.6g
Carbohydrates	6.5g
Cholesterol	–
Fat	8.9g
Sat. fats	–
Unsat. fats	–
Fiber	0

Minerals

Phosphorus	167mg
Calcium	11mg
Iron	0.4mg
Sodium	–
Potassium	–
Magnesium	–

Vitamins

A	0
B1	0.04mg
B2	0.07mg
✳ B3	1.6mg
B6	–
B12	–
Folic Acid	–
C	0
D	–
E	–

Fish sticks are known in Britain as **fish fingers**.

Fried fish cakes made with canned flaked fish, potatoes and egg have approx. the same quantity of nutrients as the frozen cooked fish sticks.

Frozen fried fish cakes have more calories (270), less protein (9.2g), more carbohydrates (17.2g), and more fat (17.9g).

GOOSE
ROAST
100g/3½oz

Only geese under 10 months old can be roasted. A young goose can be recognized by the pliability of its underbill. Young geese can be cooked and treated like turkey.

A goose older than 10 months is tough and must be braised.

Foie gras (goose liver paté) is made from the overenlarged liver of a Strasbourg- or Toulouse-raised goose which has been immobilized and then crammed almost till bursting with food.

In England, Queen Elizabeth I ordered every household to serve roast goose on September 29, Michaelmas day, to celebrate the defeat of the Spanish Armada. This custom has now died out.

146

NUTRITIONAL CONTENT	
Joules	1789.2
Calories	426
✹ Proteins	23.7g
Carbohydrates	0
✹ Cholesterol	86.8mg
✹ Fat	36g
Sat. fats	–
Unsat. fats	–
Fiber	0
Minerals	
✹ Phosphorus	240mg
Calcium	11mg
Iron	2.1mg
✹ Sodium	145mg
✹ Potassium	406mg
Magnesium	30.8mg
Vitamins	
A	–
B1	0.08mg
✹ B2	0.24mg
✹ B3	8.1mg
B6	–
B12	–
Folic Acid	–
C	–
D	–
E	–

NUTRITIONAL CONTENT

Joules	344.4
Calories	82
Proteins	1.1g
Carbohydrates	21.2g
Cholesterol	0
Fat	0.2g
Sat. fats	–
Unsat. fats	–
✸ Fiber	0.4g

Minerals

Phosphorus	32mg
Calcium	32mg
Iron	0.8mg
Sodium	2mg
Potassium	270mg
Magnesium	24mg

Vitamins

A	160iu
B1	0.08mg
B2	0.04mg
✸ B3	0.4mg
✸ B6	0.64mg
B12	0
✸ Folic Acid	4.4mcg
✸ C	76mg
D	0
E	0.6mg

Grapefruit were so called because of the way they hang in bunches like grapes. It was a Chinese custom to serve grapefruit at the beginning of the meal – a custom which has been adopted by the West.

Different varieties of grapefruit will have different amounts of vitamin A: the white-fleshed grapefruit has 20 iu per 200g while the pink- and red-fleshed varieties have 880 iu. Grapefruit pulp consists of 88 percent water.

Grapefruit juice, which is 90 percent water, contains 78 calories per 200g. There is less calcium (18mg) and more potassium (324mg).

Unsweetened canned grapefruit juice is similar to ordinary grapefruit juice except for its lack of vitamin A (only 20 iu). **Sweetened canned grapefruit juice** has more calories (106) and carbohydrates (25g).

Frozen grapefruit juice is similar to canned grapefruit juice.

Canned grapefruit segments in heavy syrup have more calories (140) and carbohydrates (35.6g).

Candied grapefruit peel contains 632 calories, 161g carbohydrates and 4.6g fiber, and very little else.

There may be slight variations in the amount of nutrients in individual products. This may occur when different varieties of grapefruit are used, or when vitamins are added by the manufacturers.

GRAPES

RAW, AMERICAN TYPE, SLIP SKIN
100g/3½oz

American "slip skin" varieties include the Concord, Delaware, Niagara, Catawba and Scuppernong. The European "adherent skin" grapes, such as the Malaga, Muscat, Thompson Seedless, Emperor, and Flame Tokay varieties, are similar to the American grape. There is more potassium (15mg), more phosphorus (8mg) and 2g more carbohydrates. There are slightly fewer calories, protein (0.6g) and fat (0.3g).

Seedless grapes canned in heavy syrup have more calories (77), 20g carbohydrates, half the calcium of fresh grapes, less potassium (105mg) and fewer vitamins.

Canned or bottled grape juice has less calories than fresh grapes (66), less protein (0.2g), less potassium (116mg), no vitamin A and slightly less of the other vitamins.

Frozen grape juice mixed with water (3 parts) has 53 calories and very few minerals and vitamins.

Canned grape juice drink (approx. 30 percent grape juice) is similar to frozen grape juice mixed with water.

NUTRITIONAL CONTENT	
Joules	289.8
Calories	69
Proteins	1.3g
✱ Carbohydrates	15.7g
Cholesterol	0
Fat	1g
Sat. fats	–
Unsat. fats	–
✱ Fiber	0.6g
Minerals	
Phosphorus	12mg
Calcium	16mg
Iron	0.4mg
Sodium	3mg
Potassium	158mg
Magnesium	13mg
Vitamins	
A	100 iu
B1	0.05mg
B2	0.03mg
✱ B3	0.3mg
✱ B6	0.08mg
B12	0
✱ Folic Acid	5-5.4mcg
C	4mg
D	0
E	0.7mg

NUTRITIONAL CONTENT

Joules	1827
Calories	435
✱ Proteins	16.3g
Carbohydrates	0
✱ Cholesterol	90mg
✱ Fat	39.6g
Sat. fats	—
Unsat. fats	—
Fiber	0

Minerals

Phosphorus	192mg
Calcium	12.7mg
✱ Iron	2.5mg
✱ Sodium	1490mg
✱ Potassium	322mg
Magnesium	17.4mg

Vitamins

A	trace
✱ B1	0.5mg
✱ B2	0.2mg
✱ B3	3.5mg
✱ B6	0.5mg
✱ B12	1 mg
✱ Folic Acid	8mcg
C	0
D	trace
E	0

Lean boiled ham without fat has 219 calories, 23g protein, 13g fat, and approx. one third more of the vitamin and mineral content found in boiled ham with fat.

Roast ham which is medium fat (26 percent fat, 74 percent lean) supplies 374 calories, 23g protein and 30g fat. It has the same calcium and phosphorus content as boiled ham and slightly more iron (3mg). The particular ham tested was less salty so it had 65mg sodium and 285mg potassium. It has 50 iu vitamin A, 0.5mg vitamin B1, 02.mg vitamin B2 and 4.6mg vitamin B3.

Canned chopped pork or ham supplies 340 calories, 15g protein, 30g fat, a large quantity of salt (1540mg sodium), less potassium (223mg), less calcium (11.8mg), less magnesium (16.6mg), less iron (1.5mg) and less phosphorus (136mg). It has, however, the same vitamin content as boiled ham.

Canned deviled ham contains 351 calories, 13.8g protein and 32g fat. It has 8mg calcium, 92mg phosphorus, and 2.1mg iron. It has no vitamin A and only 0.1mg each of the B vitamins.

Canned minced ham supplies less calories (228) but the same amount of protein and minerals as deviled ham. It has less fat (16.9g) and slightly more vitamin B: 0.2mg vitamin B2 and 0.3mg of both vitamin B1 and B3.

HONEY

STRAINED OR EXTRACTED
7 tablespoons/100g/3½oz

NUTRITIONAL CONTENT	
Joules	1276.8
Calories	304
Proteins	0.3g
✴Carbohydrates	82.3g
Cholesterol	0
Fat	0
Sat. fats	–
Unsat. fats	–
Fiber	0
Minerals	
Phosphorus	6mg
Calcium	5mg
Iron	0.5mg
Sodium	5mg
Potassium	51mg
Magnesium	2.2mg
Vitamins	
A	0
B1	trace
B2	0.05mg
B3	0.2mg
B6	0.02mg
B12	0
Folic Acid	–
C	trace
D	0
E	–

All honey is natural. It is made by the worker bees, which gather flower nectar (which contains sucrose, a form of sugar) and transport it in their honey sacs to the hive. While the nectar is being transported, the enzymes start to break down the sucrose into fructose and glucose, to be stored in open cells in the hive until the fluid becomes thick and syrupy (due to the evaporation of extra liquid in the nectar caused by the constant movement of the worker bees' wings). The honey is then sealed with wax, which is later removed by straining or by methods involving centrifugal force.

Honey contains the same sugars as refined sugar. It also contains slightly more vitamins and minerals. Honey has less calories per spoonful because it contains more water than sugar (honey has a 20% water content).

Many claims have been made justifying the use of honey in the diet; it will cure arthritis, rheumatism, sleeplessness and bed wetting. In addition, they claim it will help sexual activities and sexual potency as well as retard aging.

There is no basis scientifically or nutritionally for any of these claims.

ICE CREAM

VANILLA, APPROX. 10% FAT
2½ scoops/100g/3½oz

NUTRITIONAL CONTENT

Joules	810.6
Calories	193
Proteins	4.5g
✷ Carbohydrates	20.8g
✷ Cholesterol	45mg
✷ Fat	10.6g
Sat. fats	6g
Unsat. fats	3g plus
Fiber	0

Minerals

Phosphorus	115mg
✷ Calcium	146mg
Iron	0.1mg
Sodium	63mg
Potassium	181mg
Magnesium	14mg

Vitamins

A	408iu
B1	0.04mg
✷ B2	0.2mg
B3	0.1mg
B6	0.04mg
✷ B12	0.4mg
✷ Folic Acid	2mcg
C	1mg
D	–
E	0.31mg

There is a small amount of zinc present in ice cream.

Frozen custard is made with egg yolks. It has more fat and vitamin A than ice cream made with milk products.

The higher the fat content of an ice cream the higher the caloric value and vitamin A content; the protein, carbohydrate and mineral content will be lower.

Ice cream with a 16 percent fat content has 222 calories, 2.6g protein, 16.1g fat and 18g carbohydrates. It has half the calcium, phosphorus, sodium, and potassium of ice cream made with 10 percent fat. It has 660 iu vitamin A and slightly less vitamin B1 and B2.

Ice milk with 5 percent fat content (5.1g of fat) has 152 calories, 4.8g protein and 22.4g carbohydrate. It has half the vitamin A but the same quantity of minerals as ice cream containing 10 percent fat. The vitamin B content is also similar. There is 10.5mg cholesterol present.

Water ice has 78 calories, 32.6g of carbohydrate, and practically no protein, fat, minerals or vitamins. Water ices made with citrus fruits (orange, lemon, lime or grapefruit) will contain the additional calories, vitamins, minerals, etc., that these fruits contain.

KALE

LEAVES, BOILED AND DRAINED

100g/3½oz

NUTRITIONAL CONTENT	
Joules	163.8
Calories	39
Proteins	4.5g
Carbohydrates	6.1g
Cholesterol	0
Fat	0.7g
Sat. fats	–
Unsat. fats	–
Fiber	0
Minerals	
Phosphorus	58mg
✸ Calcium	187mg
Iron	1.6mg
Sodium	43mg
✸ Potassium	221mg
Magnesium	–
Vitamins	
✸ A	8300iu
B1	0.1mg
B2	0.18mg
✸ B3	1.6mg
B6	–
B12	–
Folic Acid	–
✸ C	93mg
D	–
E	–

Kale is a highly underrated winter vegetable with a very large vitamin A and C content.

When fresh, the leaves (which resemble spinach) are unwilted and dark blue green.

Cooked **frozen kale** has less calories (31), slightly less protein and the same large amount of vitamin A as fresh cooked kale, slightly less vitamin B3 (0.7mg) and a large amount of vitamin C (38mg).

NUTRITIONAL CONTENT

Joules	667.8
Calories	159
✱ Proteins	25.7g
Carbohydrates	0
✱ Cholesterol	375mg
Fat	5.8g
Sat. fats	—
Unsat. fats	—
Fiber	0

Minerals

✱ Phosphorus	392mg
Calcium	20.8mg
✱ Iron	7.1mg
Sodium	164mg
Potassium	164mg
Magnesium	22.4mg

Vitamins

✱ A	1000iu
B1	0
✱ B2	2mg
✱ B3	5mg
✱ B6	0.7mg
✱ B12	25mcg
✱ Folic Acid	60mcg
C	0
D	0
E	—

A fried **sheep's kidney** has 199 calories, 28g protein, 9.1g fat, more than twice the sodium, potassium and iron, and less calcium (16.6mg) and phosphorus (264mg). The vitamin content is similar but the raw sheep's kidney has a small amount of vitamin B1 and vitamin C (0.3mg and 12mg respectively).

LAMB AND MUTTON
LEG OF LAMB, ROAST (79% LEAN)
100g/3½oz

NUTRITIONAL CONTENT	
Joules	1339.8
Calories	319
☀ Proteins	23.9g
Carbohydrates	0
Cholesterol	–
☀ Fat	24g
Sat. fats	–
Unsat. fats	–
Fiber	0
Minerals	
Phosphorus	195mg
Calcium	10mg
Iron	1.6mg
Sodium	70mg
☀ Potassium	290mg
Magnesium	21mg
Vitamins	
A	trace
B1	0.14mg
☀ B2	0.25mg
☀ B3	5.2mg
B6	0.275mg
☀ B12	0.0022mg
☀ Folic Acid	3.3mcg
C	0
D	trace
E	0.8mg

Lamb is imported from so many different sources with different climates that it is no longer referred to as "spring lamb." Meat from a 3- to 5-month-old animal is called baby or milk-finished lamb. Meat from animals between 5 months and 1½ years old is called "lamb." After that the meat is known as "mutton." These meats are cooked in the same way, but mutton is tougher and needs longer cooking. An unusually large leg of lamb is probably mutton.

A 100g slice of roast leg of mutton has less calories (292), slightly more protein (25g), less fat (20g) and more iron (4.3mg). It has slightly less of the other minerals and the same amount of vitamins.

NUTRITIONAL CONTENT

Joules	1764
Calories	420
✸ Proteins	19.5g
Carbohydrates	0
✸ Cholesterol	89.9g
✸ Fat	37.3g
Sat. fats	–
Unsat. fats	–
Fiber	0

Minerals

Phosphorus	150mg
Calcium	8mg
Iron	1.1mg
Sodium	70mg
✸ Potassium	290mg
Magnesium	17mg

Vitamins

A	trace
B1	0.11mg
✸ B2	0.21mg
✸ B3	4.5mg
B6	–
B12	–
Folic Acid	–
C	0
D	–
E	0.8mg

By cutting the fat off a lamb loin chop, you reduce its caloric value when broiled to 197 calories; its fat content is 8.6g and its protein content is 28g. There is a slight vitamin and mineral increase.

A broiled mutton chop has more calories (500), more fat (45g) and the same amount of protein. The vitamin content is similar, but there is more calcium (17.8mg), more magnesium (22.8mg) and twice as much iron (2.4mg).

When the fat is cut off the chop, the calories are reduced to 271, the fat is reduced to 17.5g, and the protein content is increased to 26.5g.

A mutton chop dipped in egg and breadcrumbs and then fried has 629 calories, less protein (15.5g), but much more fat (60g) and carbohydrates (2.6g). It has slightly less vitamins and minerals.

LAMB AND MUTTON

LAMB, RIB, BROILED CHOP (53% LEAN)

100g/3½oz

NUTRITIONAL CONTENT	
Joules	2066.4
Calories	492
✸ Proteins	16.9g
Carbohydrates	0
✸ Cholesterol	89.9mg
✸ Fat	46.5g
Sat. fats	–
Unsat. fats	–
Fiber	0
Minerals	
Phosphorus	128mg
Calcium	7mg
Iron	0.8mg
Sodium	70mg
✸ Potassium	290mg
Magnesium	–
Vitamins	
A	trace
B1	0.1mg
B2	0.18mg
✸ B3	4mg
B6	–
B12	–
Folic Acid	–
C	0
D	trace
E	0.8mg

If you cut the fat off rib chops, the caloric value is reduced to 224 calories, while the protein content is 26.9g and the fat is 12g. There is a slight increase in the amount of minerals and vitamins.

NUTRITIONAL CONTENT

Joules	1570.8
Calories	374
✹ Proteins	20.7g
Carbohydrates	0
✹ Cholesterol	89.9mg
✹ Fat	31.7g
Sat. fats	—
Unsat. fats	—
Fiber	0

Minerals

Phosphorus	163mg
Calcium	9mg
Iron	1.2mg
Sodium	70mg
✹ Potassium	290mg
Magnesium	17mg

Vitamins

A	trace
B1	0.12mg
✹ B2	0.22mg
✹ B3	4.6mg
B6	—
B12	—
✹ Folic Acid	8.2mcg
C	0
D	trace
E	0.8mg

Stewing meat cut from the breast, shoulder or neck of a sheep (mutton), has 326 calories when cooked. Its protein content remains unchanged but it has 24g fat . It has less sodium (66mg), less potassium (186mg), more calcium (50mg), more magnesium (26.6mg), and more iron (6.8mg). There is a trace of vitamin A and 0.1mg vitamin B1, 0.25mg vitamin B and 4.5mg vitamin B3. (Of course these figures could be altered by the addition to the stew of various vegetables such as carrots, celery, tomatoes, potatoes, etc.)

LEEKS
BOILED (30 MINUTES)
100g/3½oz

NUTRITIONAL CONTENT	
Joules	105
Calories	25
Proteins	1.8g
Carbohydrates	4.6g
Cholesterol	0
Fat	trace
Sat. fats	–
Unsat. fats	–
✹ Fiber	1.3g
Minerals	
Phosphorus	27.5mg
✹ Calcium	60.5mg
Iron	2mg
Sodium	6.4mg
✹ Potassium	278mg
Magnesium	12.5mg
Vitamins	
A	0.04mg
B1	0.07mg
B2	0
B3	0.4mg
B6	–
B12	0
Folic Acid	–
✹ C	15mg
D	–
E	–

Leeks resemble large scallions (green onions) and, except for their roots, are totally edible. They are eaten raw or cooked, and are used in the famous vichyssoise soup.

Nero, the Roman emperor, used to have leek soup served to him every day. The Romans believed that leeks helped to maintain and preserve a deep clear voice.

The Welsh are identified with the leek; they have had it as their badge for centuries.

158

LEMON JUICE
FRESH
1 tablespoons (juice of 2 4oz lemons)/100g/3½oz

NUTRITIONAL CONTENT	
Joules	29.4
Calories	7
Proteins	0.3g
Carbohydrates	1.6g
Cholesterol	0
Fat	trace
Sat. fats	—
Unsat. fats	—
Fiber	trace

Minerals

Phosphorus	10.3mg
Calcium	8.4mg
Iron	0.14mg
Sodium	1.5mg
Potassium	142mg
Magnesium	6.6mg

Vitamins

A	0
B1	0.02mg
B2	trace
B3	0.1mg
B6	0.06mg
B12	0
✴ Folic Acid	7mcg
✴ C	50mg
D	0
E	—

Lemons are one of the few fruits that ripen better off the tree than on.

Canned unsweetened and frozen unsweetened lemon juice are similar in their nutrients to fresh lemon juice, though they may have slightly less vitamin C (45mg).

Concentrated lemon juice will have five times the strength of fresh lemon juice until diluted, when it should resemble fresh lemon juice.

Lemonade concentrate diluted with 4 parts water will have more calories and carbohydrates and very little else. The exact amount will depend on the amount of sugar or sweetener in the product.

LETTUCE

CRISP VARIETIES: ICEBERG, N.Y., GREAT LAKES
100g/3½oz

Cos and Romaine lettuces have more calories (18), more protein (1.3g), more carbohydrate (3.5g) and more fiber (0.7g). They also contain 68mg calcium, 25mg phosphorus, 1.4mg iron, slightly more potassium (264mg), and much more vitamin A (1900 iu) and C (18mg)

    Boston and Bibb-type lettuces (Butterhead) resemble Cos lettuce. Though they have slightly less calories (14) and carbohydrates (3.5g), the real difference lies in their vitamin A content (only 970 iu, half that of Cos lettuce) and vitamin C content (8mg).

NUTRITIONAL CONTENT	
Joules	54.6
Calories	13
Proteins	0.9g
Carbohydrates	2.9g
Cholesterol	0
Fat	0.9g
Sat. fats	–
Unsat. fats	–
✹ Fiber	0.5g
Minerals	
Phosphorus	22mg
Calcium	20mg
Iron	0.5mg
Sodium	9mg
Potassium	175mg
Magnesium	–
Vitamins	
A	330iu
B1	0.06mg
B2	0.06mg
B3	0.3mg
B6	0.005mg
B12	0
✹ Folic Acid	10.3mcg
C	6mg
D	0
E	0.5mg

NUTRITIONAL CONTENT

Joules	1096
Calories	261
✸ Proteins	29.5g
Carbohydrates	4g
✸ Cholesterol	434mg
✸ Fat	13.2mg
Sat. fats	–
Unsat. fats	–
Fiber	0

Minerals

✸ Phosphorus	537mg
Calcium	13mg
✸ Iron	14.2mg
Sodium	118mg
✸ Potassium	453mg
Magnesium	26mg

Vitamins

✸ A	32700iu
✸ B1	0.24mg
✸ B2	4.17mg
✸ B3	16.5mg
✸ B6	0.67mg
✸ B12	0.06mg
Folic Acid	–
✸ C	37mg
✸ D	10iu
✸ E	1.3mg

All types of cooked liver supply large amounts of iron, protein, cholesterol and vitamin A. They will also supply the normal daily requirement of B vitamins.

Fried lamb's liver is similar to calf's liver, but will have twice as much vitamin A (75,500 iu) and 17.9mg iron.

Lamb's liver and **sheep liver** will vary in the amount of vitamin A they contain; they may have as little as 10,000 iu or as much as 100,000 iu. Calf's liver varies from 3,500 iu to 35,000 iu.

Fried beef and fried hog (pig) liver are similar in their nutrients. Fried beef liver contains 229 calories, 26.4g protein, 10.6g fat, 5.3g carbohydrates, 11mg calcium, 476mg phosphorus, 8.8mg iron, 184mg sodium and 380mg potassium. The vitamin content is 53,400 iu vitamin A, 26mg vitamin B1, 4.19mg vitamin B2 and 16.5mg vitamin B3. Beef liver will vary in its vitamin A content from 10,000 iu to 60,000 iu.

Hog (pig) liver has more iron (29.1mg) and less vitamin A (14,900 iu). Its vitamin A content can vary from 5,000 iu to 2,5000 iu.

Cooked chicken livers have 165 calories, 26.5g protein, 4.4g fat and 3.1g carbohydrates. It has 11mg calcium, 159mg phosphorus, 8.5mg iron, 61mg sodium and 151mg potassium. It has 12,300 iu vitamin A, 0.17mg vitamin B1, 2.69mg vitamin B2 and 11.7mg vitamin B3.

Cooked turkey livers resemble chicken livers in their nutrients.

No liver contains very much vitamin C.

LOBSTER

BOILED

100g/3½oz

NUTRITIONAL CONTENT	
Joules	399
Calories	95
✳ Proteins	18.7g
Carbohydrates	0.3g
✳ Cholesterol	62mg
Fat	1.5g
Sat. fats	—
Unsat. fats	—
Fiber	—
Minerals	
Phosphorus	192mg
✳ Calcium	65mg
Iron	0.8mg
✳ Sodium	210mg
Potassium	180mg
Magnesium	34.3mg
Vitamins	
A	0
B1	0.1mg
B2	0.07mg
B3	1.5mg
B6	—
B12	—
Folic Acid	—
C	trace
D	—
E	—

Canned lobster has the same food value as boiled lobster.

Lobster paste and shrimp paste have the same values (see *Shrimps*, p.225).

Lobster salad made with onion, sweet pickle, celery, eggs, mayonnaise and tomatoes, has 110 calories, 10g protein, 6.4g fat, 2g carbohydrates, 36mg calcium, 95mg phosphorus, 0.9mg iron, 124mg sodium, 264mg potassium and very few B vitamins.

Lobster Newburg, prepared with butter, egg yolks, sherry, cream and lobster meat contains 194 calories, 18.5g protein, 10.6g fat, 5g carbohydrates, 87mg calcium, 192mg phosphorus, 0.9mg iron, 229mg sodium, 171mg potassium and a few B vitamins.

All lobster recipes retain the high cholesterol content food in boiled lobster.

MACARONI AND SPAGHETTI

ENRICHED, COOKED TO A FIRM STATE (8–10 MINUTES)

100g/3½oz

NUTRITIONAL CONTENT

Joules	621.6
Calories	148
Proteins	5g
✳ Carbohydrates	30.1g
Cholesterol	0
Fat	0.5g
Sat. fats	–
Unsat. fats	–
Fiber	0.1g

Minerals

Phosphorus	65mg
Calcium	11mg
Iron	1.1mg
Sodium	1mg
Potassium	79mg
Magnesium	20mg

Vitamins

A	0
B1	0.18mg
B2	0.1mg
B3	1.4mg
B6	–
B12	–
Folic Acid	–
C	0
D	0
E	0

Macaroni and spaghetti contain very little fiber. The longer it is cooked, the less nutrients pasta contains.

If cooked for 14-20 minutes, pasta contains 111 calories, 3.4g protein, 23g carbohydrate and 0.4g fat. The extra cooking time reduces the vitamin and mineral content by one quarter.

If the spaghetti or macaroni is not enriched it will contain less iron (0.5mg) and less vitamin B: vitamin B1, 0.02mg; vitamin B2, 0.02mg; vitamin B3, 0.4mg.

Cooked macaroni and cheese has 215 calories, 8.4g protein, 11g fat, 20g carbohydrates, 181mg calcium, 161mg phosphorus, 0.9mg iron, 543mg sodium and 120mg potassium. It contains 430 iu vitamin A and slightly increased amounts of vitamin B: vitamin B1, 0.10mg; vitamin B2, 0.20mg; vitamin B3, 0.9mg.

Canned macaroni and cheese has half the food value of home-cooked macaroni and cheese.

Cooked spaghetti in tomato sauce with cheese has 104 calories, 3.5g protein, 14.8g carbohydrates and 3.5g of fat. Its vitamin content is similar to that of cooked macaroni and cheese, but it has 32mg calcium, 54mg phosphorus, 0.9mg iron, 382mg sodium and 163mg potassium.

Canned spaghetti in tomato sauce has half the caloric value and half the fat, protein, calcium and phosphorus of home-cooked spaghetti in tomato sauce. It has 1.1mg iron, 15.4g carbohydrate and 1.8mg vitamin B3, but in other ways is similar to the home-cooked dish.

Spaghetti with meatballs in tomato sauce has 134 calories, 7.5g protein, 4.7g fat and 15.6g carbohydrate. The mineral content is 50mg calcium, 95mg phosphorus, 1.5mg iron, 407mg sodium and 268mg potassium. The vitamin B content is similar to that of macaroni and cheese, but it contains 640 iu vitamin A.

Canned spaghetti with meatballs in tomato sauce has less calories (103), less protein and carbohydrate (4.9g and 11.4g respectively), half the calcium and phosphorus, 1.3mg iron, 488mg sodium, 98mg potassium and slightly less vitamin A (400 iu). Its vitamin B content is half that of the home-made dish.

MALT

DRIED

100g/3½oz

Malt extract in a dried form contains the same amount of calories and vitamins. Its protein content is halved (6g), while the amount of iron is doubled (8.7mg). It has more carbohydrate (89.2g), little fiber, some calcium (48mg), phosphorus (294mg), sodium (80mg) and potassium (230mg).

164

NUTRITIONAL CONTENT

Joules	277.2
Calories	66
Proteins	0.7g
✹ Carbohydrates	16.8g
Cholesterol	0
Fat	0.4g
Sat. fats	–
Unsat. fats	–
✹ Fiber	0.9g

Minerals

Phosphorus	13mg
Calcium	10mg
Iron	0.4mg
Sodium	7mg
Potassium	189mg
Magnesium	–

Vitamins

✹ A	4800iu
B1	0.05mg
B2	0.05mg
B3	1.1mg
B6	–
B12	0
Folic Acid	–
✹ C	35mg
D	–
E	–

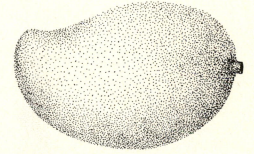

Mangoes are one of the most cultivated crops in the world. It is a vital food for millions of people in the tropics.

The mango can be as small as a plum or as large as a plate.

It has a large amount of Vitamin A and C.

Buddha himself was presented with a mango grove so that he might find rest in its cool shade.

MARGARINE

SALTED

1 tablespoon/14.3g/½oz

<table>
<tr><td colspan="2">NUTRITIONAL CONTENT</td></tr>
<tr><td>Joules</td><td>432.6</td></tr>
<tr><td>Calories</td><td>103</td></tr>
<tr><td>Proteins</td><td>0.1g</td></tr>
<tr><td>Carbohydrates</td><td>0.1g</td></tr>
<tr><td>Cholesterol</td><td>0</td></tr>
<tr><td>✹ Fat</td><td>11.5g</td></tr>
<tr><td>Sat. fats</td><td>2.6g</td></tr>
<tr><td>Unsat. fats</td><td>8.7g</td></tr>
<tr><td>Fiber</td><td>0</td></tr>
<tr><td colspan="2">Minerals</td></tr>
<tr><td>Phosphorus</td><td>2.3mg</td></tr>
<tr><td>Calcium</td><td>2.9mg</td></tr>
<tr><td>Iron</td><td>0</td></tr>
<tr><td>✹ Sodium</td><td>141.1mg</td></tr>
<tr><td>Potassium</td><td>3.3mg</td></tr>
<tr><td>Magnesium</td><td>1.3mg</td></tr>
<tr><td colspan="2">Vitamins</td></tr>
<tr><td>✹ A</td><td>471.2mg</td></tr>
<tr><td>B1</td><td>–</td></tr>
<tr><td>B2</td><td>trace</td></tr>
<tr><td>B3</td><td>trace</td></tr>
<tr><td>B6</td><td>trace</td></tr>
<tr><td>B12</td><td>–</td></tr>
<tr><td>Folic Acid</td><td>–</td></tr>
<tr><td>C</td><td>–</td></tr>
<tr><td>✹ D</td><td>43.8iu</td></tr>
<tr><td>E</td><td>–</td></tr>
</table>

Margarine was first invented in 1860 by a chef who entered a contest to discover a butter substitute.

In the United States it is usually made of refined vegetable oils which are first solidified by hydrogenation, mixed with skim milk and then reworked to add salt and remove excess water.

The solidification process used frequently turned the unsaturated fats into saturated fats, raising the cholesterol content of the margarine.

In 1960, many margarine producers claimed to have solved this problem, and now produce a low-cholesterol margarine made with polyunsaturated fats.

Margarine has approx. the same amount of calories as butter. Normally it has added vitamin A and vitamin D.

US government regulations specify the minimum amount of vitamin A (15,000 iu) which must be added to a pound of margarine.

Unsalted margarine contains less than 10mg of sodium and potassium.

Margarine in tubs is likely to have more polyunsaturated fats than margarine in stick forms because they may not be solidified.

Diet margarine usually contains water and half the amount of fats found in polyunsaturated margarines. Though usable for spreads, it cannot be used for cooking.

NUTRITIONAL CONTENT	
Joules	126
✴ Calories	30
Proteins	0.7g
Carbohydrates	7.5g
Cholesterol	0
Fat	0.1g
Sat. fats	–
Unsat. fats	–
Fiber	0.3g
Minerals	
Phosphorus	16mg
Calcium	14mg
Iron	0.4mg
Sodium	12mg
✴ Potassium	251mg
Magnesium	16mg
Vitamins	
✴ A	3400iu
B1	0.04mg
B2	0.03mg
B3	0.6mg
✴ B6	0.86mg
B12	0
✴ Folic Acid	8.4mcg
✴ C	33mg
D	0
E	0.1mg

Green-fleshed cantaloupe melon has much less vitamin A (2891 iu).

Casaba and honeydew melons have the same mineral and vitamin B content as cantaloupe melons, but they have much less vitamin A (40 iu) and less vitamin C (13 to 23mg). Honeydew melon has almost the same energy nutrients as cantaloupe, but occasionally it contains more calories (33). Casaba melon has fewer calories (27), traces of fat and a fraction less carbohydrate (6.5g).

Frozen cantaloupe and honeydew melon balls in syrup have twice the calories (62) and carbohydrate (15.7g), but have lost about one quarter of the mineral values of fresh melon. Melon balls have a large vitamin A content (1540 iu), but they lose a portion of their B vitamins (vitamin B1; 0.03mg, vitamin B2; 0.02mg, vitamin B3, 0.05mg) and some of their vitamin C (16mg).

Watermelons have much less vitamin A than cantaloupe (590 iu). They have fewer calories, carbohydrates, minerals and vitamins and only 7mg of vitamin C. They do contain more potassium.

They contain: 26 calories, 0.5g protein, 0.2g fat, 6.4g carbohydrate, 0.3g fiber, 7mg calcium, 10mg phosphorus, 0.5mg iron, 1mg sodium, 100mg potassium, 590 iu vitamin A, 0.03mg vitamin B1, 0.03mg vitamin B2, 0.2mg vitamin B3 and 7mg vitamin C.

167

MILK

FRESH WHOLE PASTEURIZED
1 cup/244g/8oz

Every cup of milk has 1mg of zinc.

Whole milk has a different vitamin content in summer and winter. Vitamin A contents can vary from 235iu in winter to 350iu in summer. Vitamin D varies from 1.5iu in winter to 3.5iu in summer. The vitamin B group content also falls in winter and rises in summer.

When **bottled milk** is left in bright light, 10 percent of its vitamin B2 content is lost every hour.

When milk is heated in an open pan, there is a 7% loss of vitamin B2. Boiling reduces the vitamin C content of milk by 12-22%.

The longer milk is stored, the less vitamin C it will have. After the first 12 hours of storage, it will have been reduced by one third, while after 24 hours, two thirds of the vitamin will have been lost.

Milk has three different proteins. When milk is boiled the skin is formed by the solidification of two of these. Milk boils over because the steam cannot escape, forcing the skin to rise.

A cup of **skim milk** has 90 calories, more calcium (316mg), 500iu vitamin A and almost no fat (0.6mg). All its other nutrients are similar to those of whole milk. It has a low cholestrol content (5mg).

Cultured buttermilk made from skim milk has more salt (257mg) than skim milk and a lower vitamin A content (81iu). It is only curdled milk.

Homogenized milk is milk in which the cream is evenly dispersed by filtering so that it will not rise to the top.

A cup of **canned evaporated milk** (undiluted) contains less vitamins but approximately double the amount of nutrients found in whole milk. It has a different taste because the process has altered two of the three milk proteins.

Dried milk is similar to fresh milk when made up, but may have lost its vitamin B and C content.

NUTRITIONAL CONTENT

Joules	627
Calories	150
Proteins	8g
✳ Carbohydrates	11g
✳ Cholesterol	33mg
✳ Fat	8g
Sat. fats	5g
Unsat. fats	3g
Fiber	0

Minerals

✳ Phosphorus	228mg
✳ Calcium	291mg
Iron	0.12mg
Sodium	120mg
✳ Potassium	370mg
Magnesium	33mg

Vitamins

A	307iu
B1	0.09mg
✳ B2	0.4mg
✳ B3	0.21mg
✳ B6	0.102mg
✳ B12	0.871mcg
✳ Folic Acid	12mcg
C	2.3mcg
✳ D	3.4iu
E	0.1mg

NUTRITIONAL CONTENT

Joules	895
Calories	213
Proteins	0
✳ Carbohydrates	55g
Cholesterol	0
Fat	0
Sat. fats	–
Unsat. fats	–
Fiber	0

Minerals

Phosphorus	84mg
✳ Calcium	684mg
✳ Iron	16.1mg
Sodium	96mg
✳ Potassium	2927mg
Magnesium	–

Vitamins

A	0
B1	0.11mg
B2	0.19mg
B3	0.2mg
B6	–
B12	–
Folic Acid	–
C	–
D	–
E	–

Molasses is a sugar byproduct. It is the residue left after the crystalization of commercial sugar from sugar cane. The sweetest molasses is left after the first sugar has been extracted. It is light in color and normally would be used for cooking, making candy or rum. Molasses from the first extraction from sugar cane has at least 252 calories, 65 carbohydrates, 165mg of calcium, 4.3mg of iron, 917mg of potassium and a small amount of B vitamins.

Some grades of molasses are reprocessed further until all the residue of the sugar is removed.

Blackstrap molasses has gone through three extractions and contains very large amounts of iron, potassium and calcium. It has an unpleasant taste and was originally used for making industrial alcohol and cattle feed. Then health food shops and health experts like Gaylord Hauser discovered it. It is now recommended as a general tonic, as well as a cure for iron and calcium deficiency during pregnancy and a help in easing menopausal discomforts. If blackstrap molasses tastes too unpleasant, dark molasses replaces it in some diets.

All **dark molasses** have a laxative effect.

English treacle is molasses. It was wisely always considered an excellent sweetener for use in the nursery.

Black treacle contains 257 calories, 67 carbohydrates, 1g of protein, 9mg of iron, 495mg of calcium, 1,470mg of potassium, 96mg of sodium and 0.4mg of copper.

MUSHROOMS

RAW

100g/3½oz

NUTRITIONAL CONTENT	
Joules	29.4
Calories	7
Proteins	1.8g
Carbohydrates	0
Cholesterol	0
Fat	trace
Sat. fats	—
Unsat. fats	—
Fiber	—
Minerals	
Phosphorus	135mg
Calcium	2.9mg
Iron	1.03mg
Sodium	9.1mg
✹ Potassium	467mg
Magnesium	13.2mg
Vitamins	
A	0
B1	0.1mg
B2	0.4mg
✹ B3	4mg
B6	0.1mg
B12	0
✹ Folic Acid	20mcg
C	3mg
D	0
E	0.1mg

Fried mushrooms have a large number of calories (217) and a good deal of fat (2.2g). There is a small increase in the mineral content: calcium 3.5mg, potassium 568mg, sodium 11mg, magnesium 16mg, phosphorus 166mg, and iron 1.25mg. There is a small decrease in the B vitamin content: B2 0.3mg, B3 0.3mg.

NUTRITIONAL CONTENT

Joules	365.4
Calories	87
✹ Proteins	16.8g
Carbohydrates	trace
Cholesterol	0
Fat	2g
Sat. fats	–
Unsat. fats	–
Fiber	–

Minerals

✹ Phosphorus	331mg
✹ Calcium	197mg
✹ Iron	13.5mg
✹ Sodium	210mg
Potassium	92mg
Magnesium	25mg

Vitamins

A	–
B1	–
B2	–
B3	–
B6	–
B12	–
Folic Acid	–
C	–
D	–
E	–

There is cholesterol in **mussels,** but the exact amount has not been determined.

Clams, which are similar to mussels, come in two types: soft-shell (steamers) and hard-shell (with little necks, or cherry stones). Clams have less nutrients than mussels. Hard-shell clams have 49 calories, 6.5g protein, 36mg cholesterol, 4.2g carbohydrates and 175mg phosphorus. Soft-shell clams are slightly richer, with 54 calories, 8.6g protein and 2g carbohydrates.

The food values of **canned clams and mussels** will change depending on what the manufacturer puts into the can. The variables include types of shell fish, salt seasoning, lemon juice, preservative and oil.

Fritters made with clams, flour, baking powder, butter and eggs contain the total of these nutrients. They have 311 calories, 11.4g protein, 15g fat, 30.9g carbohydrates, 76g calcium, 147mg potassium, and 195mg phosphorus. There is also some iron present.

NECTARINE
RAW, WEIGHED WITH STONES
100g/3½oz

NUTRITIONAL CONTENT	
Joules	194.2
Calories	46
Proteins	0.8g
✹ Carbohydrates	11.4g
Cholesterol	0
Fat	trace
Sat. fats	–
Unsat. fats	–
✹ Fiber	1g
Minerals	
Phosphorus	22mg
Calcium	3.6mg
Iron	0.42mg
Sodium	8.4mg
✹ Potassium	247mg
Magnesium	11.6mg
Vitamins	
✹ A	1650iu
B1	0
B2	0
B3	0
B6	0.02mg
B12	0
✹ Folic Acid	20.1mcg
✹ C	13mg
D	0
E	–

The **nectarines,** once referred to as "the nut of Persia," is a smooth-skinned peach. It is possible to find a nectarine growing on a peach tree, and a peach growing on a nectarine tree.

NUTRITIONAL CONTENT

Joules	525
Calories	125
Proteins	4.1g
✹ Carbohydrates	23.3
Cholesterol	–
Fat	1.5g
Sat. fats	–
Unsat. fats	–
Fiber	0.1g

Minerals

Phosphorus	59mg
Calcium	10mg
Iron	0.6mg
Sodium	2mg
Potassium	44mg
Magnesium	–

Vitamins

A	70iu
B1	0.03mg
B2	0.02mg
B3	0.4mg
B6	0.09mg
B12	–
Folic Acid	–
C	0
D	0
E	–

Enriched egg noodles, when cooked, have an additional 0.3mg iron (0.9mg in all) and a higher vitamin B content (0.14mg of B1, 0.08mg of B2, and 1.2mg of B3).

Canned fried noodles or **chow mein noodles** have a much higher calorie content (489). They have more protein (13.2g), more fat (23.5g), and much more carbohydrate content (58g).

NUTS: almonds
ROASTED AND SALTED
28.5g/1oz

NUTRITIONAL CONTENT	
Joules	752
Calories	179
✳ Proteins	5.3g
✳ Carbohydrates	5.5g
Cholesterol	0
✳ Fat	16.5g
Sat. fats	1.4g
Unsat. fats	15g
✳ Fiber	0.7g
Minerals	
✳ Phosphorus	144mg
✳ Calcium	67mg
✳ Iron	1.3mg
Sodium	56mg
✳ Potassium	184mg
✳ Magnesium	77mg
Vitamins	
A	0
B1	0.01mg
✳ B2	0.26mg
✳ B3	1mg
B6	0.03mg
B12	0
Folic Acid	0
C	trace
D	0
✳ E	2.1mg

The content of **dried almonds** is very similar to that of roasted almonds. An ounce would have a few less calories (171), one gram less fat (15.4g), much less sodium (4mg) and more vitamin B1 (0.24mg).

An ounce of **sugar-coated almonds** has less calories (130), less protein (2g), less fat (5g) and more carbohydrates (21g). It has 38mg calcium, 40mg phosphorus, 3mg iron, 6mg sodium, 73mg potassium, and 0.05mg, 0.27mg, and 1mg of vitamins B1, B2 and B3 respectively.

1oog of **defatted almond meal** contains 408 calories, 39.5g protein, 18g fat, 29g carbohydrates, 2.3g fiber, 424mg calcium, 914mg phosphorus, 8.5mg iron, 7mg sodium, 1400mg potassium, and almost twice the vitamin B content of roasted almonds.

NUTRITIONAL CONTENT

Joules	769
Calories	183
✹ Proteins	3.9g
Carbohydrates	1.2g
Cholesterol	0
✹ Fat	19g
Sat. fats	4g
Unsat. fats	14g
✹ Fiber	1g

Minerals
✹ Phosphorus	168mg
✹ Calcium	50mg
Iron	0.8mg
Sodium	0.4mg
✹ Potassium	216mg
✹ Magnesium	117mg

Vitamins
A	0
✹ B1	0.3mg
B2	0.03mg
B3	0.5mg
B6	0.3mg
B12	—
✹ Folic Acid	1mcg
C	trace
D	0
✹ E	6mg

Brazil nuts are the fruit of the Berholettia tree which grows mainly in Brazil and other South American countries.

They are 3-sided in shape and have a white, meaty kernel. There are many types of brazil nuts, but the more delicate nuts are not transported since they do not survive shipping.

In France, they are called American chestnuts.

NUTS: cashew

RAW
28.5g/1oz

NUTRITIONAL CONTENT	
Joules	673
Calories	160
✴ Proteins	5g
✴ Carbohydrates	84g
Cholesterol	0
✴ Fat	13g
Sat. fats	2g
Unsat. fats	10g
✴ Fiber	0.4g
Minerals	
✴ Phosphorus	107mg
Calcium	11mg
✴ Iron	1mg
Sodium	4mg
✴ Potassium	133mg
✴ Magnesium	76mg
Vitamins	
A	29iu
B1	0.12mg
B2	0.07mg
B3	0.5mg
B6	–
B12	–
Folic Acid	–
C	0
D	0
✴ E	1.7mg

Salted cashew nuts have approx. 200mg of sodium per 100g (or 57mg per ounce).

Cashews, like all nuts, contain a great deal of unsaturated fatty acid, most of which is oleic acid.

NUTRITIONAL CONTENT

Joules	437
Calories	104
Proteins	1.1g
Carbohydrates	1.1g
Cholesterol	0
✴ Fat	10.2g
Sat. fats	8.5g
Unsat. fats	0.5g
✴ Fiber	1.14g

Minerals

Phosphorus	27mg
Calcium	3.7mg
Iron	0.59mg
Sodium	4.7mg
✴ Potassium	124mg
Magnesium	14.8mg

Vitamins

A	0
B1	0.008mg
B2	0.005mg
B3	0.09mg
B6	0.02mg
B12	0
✴ Folic Acid	8mcg
C	trace
D	0
E	–

Dried coconut has 178 calories, 1.1g protein, 10g fat and 1g carbohydrate. It will have almost twice the sodium content (8.1mg), potassium (214mg), calcium (6.4mg), magnesium (26mg), iron (1.02mg) and phosphorus (46mg). It will have approx. the same vitamin content as fresh coconut.

If it is sweetened, some of the coconut is replaced by sugar, causing the fat content to decrease and the carbohydrate content to increase. There will be less vitamins and minerals (sugar doesn't have any).

An ounce of coconut milk has no calories, practically no protein (0.1g), no fat, and 1.4g of carbohydrate. It has a high sodium content (30mg), 89mg of potassium, 8mg of calcium, practically no iron or phosphorus and a very slight trace of the B vitamins.

Coconut has less protein than other nuts, and is unique in having a very high saturated fatty acid content. Ounce for ounce more than milk.

The saturated fatty acid in coconut meat contains a high proportion of lauric acid, which is liquid at room temperature. Because of this property it is used to make articial milk and modified cow's milk products.

Those who have been warned away from high saturated fat products like cow's milk, cheese and other dairy products should check the artificial milk products to ensure that coconut oil is not one of the major ingredients.

NUTS: hazel

RAW

28.5g/1oz

NUTRITIONAL CONTENT

Joules	760
Calories	181
✷ Proteins	3.6g
✷ Carbohydrates	5g
Cholesterol	0
✷ Fat	17.8g
Sat. fats	0.8g
Unsat. fats	13g
✷ Fiber	0.8g

Minerals

✷ Phosphorus	96mg
✷ Calcium	59.7mg
✷ Iron	0.9mg
Sodium	0.5mg
✷ Potassium	201mg
✷ Magnesium	52.6

Vitamins

A	0
✷ B1	0.13mg
B2	–
B3	0.2mg
B6	0.16mg
B12	0
✷ Folic Acid	17.7mg
C	0
D	0
✷ E	8mg

Hazel nuts are rich in oil.

They are the fruit of the hazelnut or cob nut tree and are grown both in the United States and Europe.

In Europe cultivated hazelnuts are called filberts or noisettes.

NUTRITIONAL CONTENT

Joules	703.5
Calories	167.14
✳ Proteins	7.4g
✳ Carbohydrates	5.4g
Cholesterol	0
✳ Fat	14.2g
Sat. fats	3g
Unsat. fats	6g
✳ Fiber	0.7g

Minerals
✳ Phosphorus	114.6mg
Calcium	21.5mg
Iron	0.6mg
✳ Sodium	119mg
✳ Potassium	193mg
✳ Magnesium	50mg

Vitamins
A	0
B1	0.09mg
B2	0.04mg
✳ B3	5mg
B6	–
B12	–
Folic Acid	–
C	0
D	0
E	–

Peanuts are highly nutritious.

If no salt has been added to roasted peanuts, they have a very low sodium-salt content (5mg).

Peanuts roasted in their skins are nutritionally similar to peanuts roasted without their skins.

An ounce of **peanut butter** made with a small amount of fat and salt will have no more calories than an ounce of roasted peanuts (166), less calcium (18mg), more salt (173mg) and less vitamin B1 (0.04 mg). It will still have a large amount of protein (8g), fat (14g) and carbohydrate (5g). A manufacturer may add large amounts of fat, salt and a sweetener. In that case, the energy nutrients (fats, carbohydrates and proteins) will increase, as will the amounts of calories they contain. The mineral and vitamin content will not greatly increase.

An ounce of **peanut spread** (nutritionally a form of peanut butter) has 171 calories, 6g protein, 15g fat, 6g carbohydrates, 0.4g fiber, 14mg calcium, 92mg phosphorus, 0.4mg iron, 171mg sodium, 151mg potassium and less vitamin B than roasted peanuts.

100g of **defatted peanut flour** has 371 calories, 47g protein, 9g fat, 31g carbohydrates, 2.7g fiber, almost no sodium (9mg), a good deal of potassium (1,186mg), a large amount of calcium (104mg) and phosphorus (720mg) and iron (3.5mg). It has 0.75 vitamin B1, 0.22mg vitamin B2, and 28mg vitamin B3.

An ounce of **chocolate-coated peanuts** has 160 calories, 4.6g protein, 12g fat, and 11g carbohydrates.

An ounce of **peanut brittle** has 120 calories, 23g carbohydrates, 2g protein, 3g fat and a very small amount of vitamins and minerals.

Peanuts are also called goobers, pinders, ground nuts and earth nuts.

NUTS: pecan

RAW

28.5g/1oz

NUTRITIONAL CONTENT	
Joules	824
Calories	196
✸ Proteins	3g
✸ Carbohydrates	4g
Cholesterol	0
✸ Fat	20g
Sat. fats	1.4g
Unsat. fats	17g
✸ Fiber	0.7g
Minerals	
✸ Phosphorus	83mg
Calcium	21mg
Iron	0.7mg
Sodium	trace
✸ Potassium	172mg
✸ Magnesium	142mg
Vitamins	
A	37iu
B1	0.2mg
B2	0.04mg
B3	0.3mg
B6	–
B12	–
Folic Acid	–
C	0.6mg
D	–
E	–

Pecan nuts come from the pecan tree, a type of hickory tree, which is native to the United States.

Some species of the pecan nut have been developed with paper-thin shells.

A pecan can absorb up to 75% of its weight in oil.

NUTRITIONAL CONTENT

Joules	713
Calories	170
✸ Proteins	6g
✸ Carbohydrates	5.4g
Cholesterol	0
✸ Fat	15.3g
Sat. fats	1g
Unsat. fats	13g
✸ Fiber	0.5g

Minerals

✸ Phosphorus	143mg
Calcium	37.4mg
✸ Iron	2mg
Sodium	0
✸ Potassium	278mg
✸ Magnesium	45mg

Vitamins

A	66iu
✸ B1	0.2mg
B2	0
B3	0.4mg
B6	–
B12	–
Folic Acid	–
C	0
D	0
✸ E	1.5mg

Pistachio nuts are very small green seeds, loved for their color and flavor.

They are grown in Iran, Syria, Afghanistan, Italy and Sicily. They are also grown in the southwestern United States and in Mexico.

NUTS: walnuts

WITHOUT SHELLS

28.5g/1oz

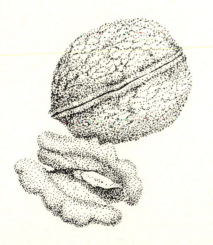

Unripe walnuts contain a great deal of vitamin C.

NUTRITIONAL CONTENT	
Joules	655.2
Calories	156
✹Proteins	3.6g
Carbohydrates	1.4g
Cholesterol	0
✹Fat	14.6g
Sat. fats	1g
Unsat. fats	5.2g
✹Fiber	1.5g
Minerals	
✹Phosphorus	145mg
Calcium	17.3mg
Iron	0.7mg
Sodium	0.8mg
✹Potassium	195mg
✹Magnesium	37mg
Vitamins	
A	0
✹B1	0.1mg
B2	0.04mg
B3	0.3mg
✹B6	0.3mg
B12	0
✹Folic Acid	22mcg
C	trace
D	0
✹E	6mg

NUTRITIONAL CONTENT

Joules	126
Calories	30
Proteins	0.3g
Carbohydrates	0.3g
Cholesterol	0
Fat	3.1g
Sat. fats	—
Unsat. fats	—
✳ Fiber	3g

Minerals

Phosphorus	4.8mg
Calcium	26mg
✳ Iron	6.2mg
✳ Sodium	639mg
Potassium	26mg
Magnesium	17.4mg

Vitamins

A	trace
B1	trace
B2	trace
B3	—
B6	0.01mg
B12	0
Folic Acid	0.3mcg
C	0
D	0
E	0

Olives are the goddess Athena's gift to mankind. She won an island from the sea god Poseidon by presenting its islanders with the gift which would be of the greatest benefit to them — an olive tree. Olives are said to have been first cultivated 6,000 years ago.

Untreated olives, whether green and unripe or black and sun-ripened, are bitter. They must first be soaked in water and then in brine before they become palatable.

Ripened black olives are less salty and contain very little vitamin A. They have slightly more carbohydrates, fats and calories. An ounce of black olives contains approx. 37 calories, 4g fat and 0.7g carbohydrates. It has 232mg sodium and 17iu vitamin A, with traces of the B vitamins.

Greek olives are black, salted and kept in oil or oil-coated. They are thus much saltier and richer than other olives. They contain 97 calories, 6g protein, 10g fat, 2.5g carbohydrates, 1g fiber and 939g sodium.

ONIONS

RAW

100g/3½oz

Boiled onions lose some of their calories (29) and carbohydrates (6.5g). They also lose a very small portion of their minerals.

Dehydrated flaked onions have 380 calories, 9g protein, 4g fiber and 82g carbohydrate. Their vitamin content includes a large amount of potassium (1,383mg), which decreases rapidly when the onions are wet, and 166mg calcium, 273mg phosphorus, 2.9mg iron and 88mg sodium. They have approx. five times the vitamin content of raw onions.

Fried onions have 355 calories, 10g carbohydrate, 33g fat and 2g protein. They increase in mineral content; the quantities are 20mg sodium, 267mg potassium, 61mg calcium, 0.5mg iron, 14.8mg magnesium and 59mg phosphorus. Their vitamin content rises a little also.

Small young green raw onions, also known as **scallions** or **spring onions,** contain, in the bulb and the white portion of their tops, 45 calories, 1.1g protein, 10.5g carbohydrate, 1g fiber and very little fat. They have more calcium (40mg) and potassium (231mg) and vitamin C (25mg) than raw onions. They have half the amount of sodium and scant vitamin A.

NUTRITIONAL CONTENT	
Joules	160
Calories	38
Proteins	1.5g
Carbohydrates	9g
Cholesterol	0
Fat	0.1g
Sat. fats	–
Unsat. fats	–
✹ Fiber	0.6g
Minerals	
Phosphorus	36mg
Calcium	27mg
Iron	0.5mg
Sodium	10mg
Potassium	157mg
Magnesium	12mg
Vitamins	
A	40iu
B1	0.03mg
B2	0.04mg
B3	0.2mg
B6	0.1mg
B12	0
✹ Folic Acid	10mcg
✹ C	10mg
D	0
E	0.3mg

184

NUTRITIONAL CONTENT

Joules	206
Calories	49
Proteins	1g
✸ Carbohydrates	12.2g
Cholesterol	0
Fat	0.2g
Sat. fats	—
Unsat. fats	—
✸ Fiber	0.5g

Minerals

Phosphorus	20mg
Calcium	41mg
Iron	0.4mg
Sodium	1mg
✸ Potassium	200mg
Magnesium	11mg

Vitamins

A	200iu
B1	0.1mg
B2	0.04mg
B3	0.4mg
B6	0.03mg
B12	0
✸ Folic Acid	5mcg
✸ C	50mg
D	0
E	0.2mg

Fresh orange juice has, in 100ml or 3½ fluid oz, almost the same energy nutrients as the whole fruit: 45 calories, 0.7g protein, 0.2g fat, 10.4g carbohydrate and 0.1g fiber. It resembles the fresh fruit in its sodium, potassium and vitamin content but has less calcium (11mg), less phosphorus (17mg) and 0.2mg iron.

All varieties of orange juice tend to be similar in their nutrients. **Canned sweetened orange juice** has 7 calories more than fresh orange juice and all canned orange juice has 10mg less vitamin C. Otherwise all canned frozen diluted, canned concentrated diluted orange juices have the same amount of nutrition.

Orange juice drink has 50 calories, 12.7g carbohydrate, and practically no fat, protein, fiber or minerals. It contains 580iu vitamin A, almost no vitamin B and 16mg vitamin C. However these values may be altered by the individual manufacturer.

Candied orange peel has 316 calories, 81g carbohydrate, very little protein (0.4g) and fat (0.3g) and nothing else.

OYSTERS
RAW

7 oysters/100g/3½oz

NUTRITIONAL CONTENT	
Joules	277
Calories	66
✴ Proteins	8.4g
Carbohydrates	1.8g
✴ Cholesterol	53mg
Fat	1.8g
Sat. fats	–
Unsat. fats	–
Fiber	–
Minerals	
Phosphorus	143mg
Calcium	94mg
✴ Iron	5.5mg
Sodium	73mg
Potassium	121mg
Magnesium	32mg
Vitamins	
A	310iu
B1	0.14mg
B2	0.18mg
B3	2.5mg
B6	0.03mg
✴ B12	15mcg
Folic Acid	trace
C	trace
D	trace
E	–

Pacific and Olympia oysters have slightly more nutrients: 91 calories, 10.6g protein, 2.2g fat, 6.4g carbohydrates, and more vitamin C (30mg).

Fried oysters, which are oysters dipped in egg, milk and bread crumbs, then fried in vegetable oil, are very rich. They have 239 calories, 19g carbohydrates and 13.9g fat. Their mineral and vitamin content increases as well. The mineral content consists of 152mg calcium, 241mg phosphorus, 8mg iron, 206mg sodium, 203mg potassium. The vitamin content is 440iu vitamin A, 17mg B1, 29mg B2, and 3.2mg B3.

Oyster stew made with two parts milk to one part oysters increases the calorie content to 97, the fat content to 6.4g, the carbohydrates to 4.5g, the calcium to 114mg, and the sodium to 339mg.

NUTRITIONAL CONTENT	
Joules	277
Calories	66
Proteins	1.5g
✹ Carbohydrates	14.9g
Cholesterol	0
Fat	0.5g
Sat. fats	–
Unsat. fats	–
✹ Fiber	2g
Minerals	
Phosphorus	62mg
Calcium	45mg
Iron	0.6mg
Sodium	8mg
✹ Potassium	379mg
Magnesium	–
Vitamins	
A	30iu
B1	0.07mg
B2	0.08mg
B3	0.1mg
B6	0.1mg
B12	0
Folic Acid	–
✹ C	10mg
D	0
E	0

Parsnips are a root vegetable, belonging to the carrot family, which has been cultivated since Roman times. Wine and beer have sometimes been made of parsnips. Like all root vegetables, they tend to produce flatulence.

PEACHES

RAW

1 medium/100g/3½oz

White-fleshed peaches have much less vitamin A (about 50iu per 100g).

Peaches canned in heavy syrup have twice the calories (78), twice the carbohydrates (20g) and sodium (2mg) of raw peaches. They have less protein (0.4g), less calcium (4mg), phosphorus (12mg), potassium (130mg), vitamin A (430iu), vitamin C (3mg) and half the B vitamins.

Peaches canned in water with artificial sweetener or no sweetener have less calories (31g), less protein (0.4g), less calcium (4mg), phosphorus (13mg), potassium (137mg), vitamin A (430iu), vitamin C (3mg) and half the B vitamins.

Frozen sweetened peaches contain the same nutrients as peaches canned in heavy syrup, but they have more vitamin A (650iu) and vitamin C (40mg). The sugar increases their calories to 88 and their carbohydrates to 22.6g.

Cooked dried peaches which have been sulfured have 82 calories, 1mg protein, 0.2g fat and 21.4g carbohydrate. They have 1g fiber, 15mg calcium, 37mg phosphorus, 1.9mg iron, 5mg sodium, 297mg potassium, 1220iu vitamin A, 0.06mg vitamin B2, 1.5mg vitamin B3 and very little vitamin C (2mg).

If sugar is added the vitamin A content decreases (1070iu) and the mineral content drops by one seventh, while the calories increase (110) as do the carbohydrates (31g).

Cooked dehydrated sulfured peach pieces cooked with added sugar have the same nutritional content as dried cooked peaches with added sugar.

Canned peach nectar containing 40 percent fruit has 48 calories, 12g carbohydrates, and practically no minerals or vitamins except for 430iu vitamin A.

NUTRITIONAL CONTENT	
Joules	160
Calories	38
Proteins	0.6g
✴ Carbohydrates	9.7g
Cholesterol	0
Fat	0.1g
Sat. fats	—
Unsat. fats	—
✴ Fiber	0.6g
Minerals	
Phosphorus	19mg
Calcium	9mg
Iron	0.5mg
Sodium	1mg
✴ Potassium	202mg
Magnesium	10mg
Vitamins	
✴ A	1330iu
B1	0.02mg
B2	0.05mg
B3	1mg
B6	0.024mg
B12	0
✴ Folic Acid	2.3mcg
C	7mg
D	0
E	0

NUTRITIONAL CONTENT

Joules	256
Calories	61
Proteins	0.7g
✸ Carbohydrates	15.3g
Cholesterol	0
Fat	0.4g
Sat. fats	—
Unsat. fats	—
✸ Fiber	1.4g

Minerals
Phosphorus	11mg
Calcium	8mg
Iron	0.3mg
Sodium	2mg
Potassium	130mg
Magnesium	7mg

Vitamins
A	20iu
B1	0.02mg
B2	0.04mg
B3	0.1mg
B6	0.017mg
B12	0
✸ Folic Acid	2.3mcg
C	4mg
D	0
E	0.5mg

Candied pears have 303 calories, 76g carbohydrates, a little protein (1.3g), less fat (0.6g) and nothing else.

Canned peeled pears in water, with or without sweetener, have half the calories of raw pears (32), less than half the protein (0.2g), and half the fiber and carbohydrates (8.3g). The mineral content is greatly reduced as is the vitamin content. These pears are eaten for enjoyment alone.

Canned pears in heavy syrup have 76 calories, 0.2g protein, 0.2g fat and 20g carbohydrates. They have the same drastically reduced vitamin and mineral content as canned pears in water.

Cooked dried sulfured pears with no added sugar have twice the nutritive value of raw pears, including most vitamins and minerals except for sodium (only 3mg), vitamin A (30iu) and vitamin C (2mg).

When sugar is added the calorie count increases to 151 calories, the carbohydrates to 38g, and the phosphorus (20mg) and potassium (244mg) decrease.

Pear nectar containing 40 percent fruit has 52 calories and 13g carbohydrates but very little of anything else, including vitamins.

PEAS: green

RAW
100g/3½oz

Boiled and drained fresh peas lose some of their natural "goodness" when cooked. They lose 13 calories while retaining 71 calories. They also lose one gram of protein, and 2 grams of carbohydrates. They have 17g less phosphorus (99mg), 3mg less calcium (23mg), 1mg less sodium and 120mg less potassium (196mg). 540iu vitamin A remain after cooking. Some vitamin B will be lost, leaving 0.28mg of B1, 0.11mg of B2 and 2.3mg of B3. 20mg of vitamin C will be left.

Canned drained cooked peas have 88 calories, 4.7mg protein, 16.8g carbohydrates, 26mg calcium, 2.3g fiber, 76mg phosphorus, 1.9mg iron, 236mg sodium, 96mg potassium, 690mg vitamin A, 0.09mg vitamin B1, 0.06mg B2, 0.8mg B3 and 8mg of vitamin C.

Canned low-sodium dietary peas will differ in the amount of sodium they contain (usually 2-3mg).

Canned sweet peas (sugar peas) have almost the same nutrient values as regular canned drained peas. They may have slightly fewer calories (80) and less carbohydrate (15g).

Frozen peas, when boiled and drained, have 68 calories, 5g protein, 12g carbohydrates, 1.9g fiber, 19mg calcium, 86mg phosphorus, 1.9mg iron, 115mg sodium, 135mg potassium, 600iu vitamin A, 0.27mg vitamin B1, 0.09mg vitamin B2, 1.7mg vitamin B3 and 13mg vitamin C.

Dried split peas, soaked and cooked, have 115 calories, 8g protein, 0.3g fat, 21g carbohydrates, 0.4g fiber, 11mg calcium, 89mg phosphorus, 1.7mg iron, 13mg sodium, 296mg potassium, 40iu of vitamin A, 0.15mg vitamin B1, 0.09mg vitamin B2 and 0.9mg vitamin B3.

Frozen peas and carrots when cooked have 53 calories, 3.2g protein, 0.3g fat, 10.1g carbohydrates and 1.5g fiber. They contain 25mg calcium, 57mg phosphorus, 1.1mg iron, 84mg sodium, 157mg potassium, 9300iu vitamin A, 0.19mg vitamin B1, 0.07mg B2, 1.3mg B3 and 8mg vitamin C.

NUTRITIONAL CONTENT	
Joules	353
Calories	84
Proteins	6.3g
✸ Carbohydrates	14.4g
Cholesterol	0
Fat	0.4g
Sat. fats	–
Unsat. fats	–
✸ Fiber	2g
Minerals	
Phosphorus	116mg
Calcium	26mg
Iron	1.9mg
Sodium	2mg
✸ Potassium	316mg
Magnesium	35mg
Vitamins	
A	640iu
✸ B1	0.35mg
B2	0.14mg
✸ B3	2.9mg
B6	0.16mg
B12	0
✸ Folic Acid	35.5mcg
✸ C	27mg
D	0
✸ E	2.1mg

190

NUTRITIONAL CONTENT

Joules	181
Calories	43
Proteins	2.9g
✳ Carbohydrates	9.5g
Cholesterol	0
Fat	0.2g
Sat. fats	–
Unsat. fats	–
✳ Fiber	1.2g

Minerals

Phosphorus	76mg
Calcium	56mg
Iron	0.5mg
Sodium	0
Potassium	119mg
Magnesium	–

Vitamins

A	610iu
B1	0.22mg
B2	0.11mg
B3	–
B6	–
B12	–
Folic Acid	–
C	14mg
D	–
E	–

Mangetout are sometimes called **sugar** or **snow peas.** Their pods have no parchment lining and therefore the whole vegetable, both pods and peas, can be eaten.

If eaten **raw,** they will contain slightly more calories (55), carbohydrates (12g), potassium (170mg) and vitamin C (21cg).

191

PEPPERS: green (sweet)

RAW

100g/3½oz

NUTRITIONAL CONTENT

Joules	92.4
Calories	22
Proteins	1.2g
Carbohydrates	4.8g
Cholesterol	0
Fat	0.2g
Sat. fats	–
Unsat. fats	–
✹ Fiber	1.4g

Minerals

Phosphorus	22mg
Calcium	9mg
Iron	0.7mg
Sodium	13mg
✹ Potassium	213mg
Magnesium	–

Vitamins

A	420iu
B1	0.08mg
B2	0.08mg
B3	0.5mg
B6	0.26mg
B12	0
✹ Folic Acid	9.8mcg
✹ C	128mg
D	0
E	0.7mg

When **peppers** are boiled they lose a small portion of their nutrients, the amount of calories is reduced to 18, of carbohydrates to 3.8g, of phosphorus to 16mg and of potassium to 149mg. There is a slight reduction in iron (0.5mg) and in vitamin B1 to 0.06mg, in vitamin B2 to 0.07mg and in soluble vitamin C to 96mg.

If a **green pepper** is stuffed with beef and bread crumbs and then cooked, it gains in calories (170), in protein (13g), fat (5.5g) and carbohydrates (17g). The increased minerals are calcium (42mg), phosphorus (121mg), iron (2.1mg), sodium (314mg) and potassium (258mg). There is less vitamin A (280iu) and only 0.09mg vitamin B1, 0.17mg vitamin B2, 2.5mg vitamin B3 and 40mg vitamin C.

Raw **red peppers** contain a good deal of vitamin A (4450iu) and of vitamin C (204mg). They have slightly more carbohydrates and minerals (7.1g carbohydrates) and 31 calories.

Pimentos – the large red sweet Spanish peppers – when canned have a large amount of vitamin A (2300iu) and vitamin C (95mg). They have 27 calories, 0.9g protein, 5.8g carbohydrates, 1.7mg iron and very little of any other mineral. They contain only a trace of the B vitamins.

PERSIMMONS
JAPANESE (KAKI)
100g/3½oz

NUTRITIONAL CONTENT

Joules	323.4
Calories	77
Proteins	0.7g
✹ Carbohydrates	19.7g
Cholesterol	0
Fat	0.4g
Sat. fats	–
Unsat. fats	–
✹ Fiber	1.6g

Minerals

Phosphorus	26mg
Calcium	6mg
Iron	0.3mg
Sodium	6mg
✹ Potassium	174mg
Magnesium	8mg

Vitamins

✹ A	2710iu
B1	0.03mg
B2	0.02mg
B3	0.1mg
B6	–
B12	–
Folic Acid	–
✹ C	66mg
D	–
E	–

Native **persimmons** have more calories (127) and more carbohydrates (33.5g). They have more calcium (27mg), more iron (2.5mg), more potassium (310mg) and vitamin C (66mg). They have only 1mg of sodium.

193

PICKLES (CUCUMBER)

DILL
100g/3½oz

NUTRITIONAL CONTENT	
Joules	46.2
Calories	11
Proteins	0.7g
Carbohydrates	2.2g
Cholesterol	0
Fat	0.2g
Sat. fats	—
Unsat. fats	—
✹ Fiber	0.5g
Minerals	
Phosphorus	21mg
Calcium	26mg
Iron	1mg
✹ Sodium	1428mg
✹ Potassium	200mg
Magnesium	12mg
Vitamins	
A	100iu
B1	trace
B2	0.02mg
B3	trace
B6	0.007mg
B12	—
Folic Acid	—
C	6mg
D	—
E	—

Sour pickles are like dill pickles but they lack potassium. They also have less calcium (17mg) and less phosphorus (16mg). They contain an enormous amount of salt (1353mg), which is still less than dill pickles. They have more iron (3.2mg).

Bread and butter pickles have more calories (73), carbohydrates (17.9g) and vitamin A (140iu). They have much less sodium (673mg), no potassium and little iron (1.8mg).

Sweet pickles have 146 calories and 36.5g carbohydrates. They have very little calcium (12mg), phosphorus (16mg) or vitamin A (90iu). They contain similar amounts of iron but no sodium or potassium.

Sour relish resembles dill pickles but contains more calories (19).

Sweet relish has 138 calories, 0.5g protein, 0.6g fat, 34g carbohydrates. It has less calcium (20mg), less phosphorus (14mg) and iron (0.8mg), and 712mg sodium.

194

NUTRITIONAL CONTENT

Joules	218.4
Calories	52
Proteins	0.4g
✷ Carbohydrates	13.7g
Cholesterol	0
Fat	0.2g
Sat. fats	–
Unsat. fats	–
✷ Fiber	0.4g

Minerals

Phosphorus	8mg
Calcium	17mg
Iron	0.5mg
Sodium	1mg
Potassium	146mg
Magnesium	–

Vitamins

A	70iu
B1	0.09mg
B2	0.03mg
B3	0.2mg
B6	0.088mg
B12	0
✷ Folic Acid	5.9mcg
✷ C	17mg
D	0
E	–

Candied pineapple is mostly carbohydrates (80g) and supplies lots of calories (316). It has a little protein (0.8g) and fat (0.4g), and that's all.

Canned pineapple in water which contains artificial sweetener, if any, has a reduced proportion of all food nutrients. It has 39 calories, 0.3g protein, 0.1g fat and 10.2g carbohydrates. It has very little mineral content: calcium, 12mg; phosphorus, 5mg; iron, 0.3mg; sodium, 1mg; potassium, 99mg. It also has very few vitamins: vitamin A, 50iu; vitamin B1, 0.08mg; vitamin B2, 0.02mg; vitamin B3, 0.2mg; and vitamin C, 7mg.

Canned pineapple in heavy syrup has 74 calories, very little protein (0.3g) or fat (0.1g), a large number of carbohydrates (19.4g) and 0.3g fiber. The vitamin and mineral content is almost identical to that of canned pineapple in water. (It is the canning process which occasions the loss of the vitamins, not the syrup that the fruit is canned in.)

Canned unsweetened pineapple juice is similar to raw pineapple in the nutrients it contains. It has 50iu vitamin A and 9mg vitamin C.

Frozen chunks of pineapple have 85 calories, 22.2g carbohydrates, 0.4g protein, 0.1g fat and low mineral content: calcium, 9mg; phosphorus, 4mg; sodium, 2mg; potassium, 100mg; iron, 0.4mg. Its vitamin content is also very low.

Defrosted unsweetened pineapple juice diluted with three parts water is similar in nutrients to the raw fruit. It will have less vitamin A (10iu) and vitamin C (12mg) and slightly less calcium (11mg).

Canned pineapple and orange juice drink is similar to diluted frozen pineapple juice and canned pineapple and grapefruit juice drink, except that it has more vitamin A (50iu).

PIZZA
WITH CHEESE
¼ small pizza/100g/3½oz

NUTRITIONAL CONTENT	
Joules	991.2
Calories	236
✳ Proteins	12g
✳ Carbohydrates	28.3g
✳ Cholesterol	18mg
✳ Fat	8.3g
Sat. fats	3g
Unsat. fats	5g
✳ Fiber	0.3g
Minerals	
Phosphorus	195mg
✳ Calcium	221mg
Iron	1mg
✳ Sodium	702mg
Potassium	130mg
Magnesium	–
Vitamins	
✳ A	630iu
B1	0.06mg
✳ B2	0.2mg
B3	1mg
B6	–
B12	–
Folic Acid	–
C	8mg
D	–
E	–

This pizza is made with flour, yeast, olive oil, milk, mozzarella cheese and some tomato sauce.

With just sausage and very little cheese, a pizza would have less calories (234), less protein (7.8g), 9.3g fat and 29.6g carbohydrates. It would have much less calcium (17mg), less phosphorus (92mg), more iron (1.2mg), more sodium (729mg) and more potassium (168mg). There would be fewer vitamins: vitamin A, 560iu; vitamin B1, 0.09mg; vitamin B2, 0.12mg; vitamin B3, 1.5 mg; vitamin C, 9mg.

NUTRITIONAL CONTENT

Joules	231
Calories	66
Proteins	0.5g
✳ Carbohydrates	17.8g
Cholesterol	0
Fat	trace
Sat. fats	—
Unsat. fats	—
✳ Fiber	0.4g

Minerals

Phosphorus	17mg
Calcium	18mg
Iron	0.5mg
Sodium	2mg
✳ Potassium	299mg
Magnesium	9mg

Vitamins

A	300iu
B1	0.08mg
B2	0.03mg
B3	0.5mg
B6	0.05mg
B12	0
Folic Acid	0.6–2.9mcg
C	4–6mg
D	0
E	0.7mg

Japanese and hybrid plums have less calories (48) and 12.3g carbohydrates. They have slightly more fat (0.2g) and fiber (0.6g), and approximately the same amount of minerals, though less potassium, 170mg. They have 250iu vitamin A and less vitamin B1 (0.03mg).

Prune-type plums have more calories (75) and 19g carbohydrates. They have the same mineral and vitamin content as Japanese and hybrid plums.

Canned greengage plums in water have half the calories, carbohydrates, fiber, calcium, sodium, potassium and vitamins that fresh damson plums have. They have a minimum of protein (0.4g) and fat (0.2g).

Canned purple Italian prune-type plums in heavy syrup have 83 calories, 0.4g protein, 0.1g fat, 21.6g carbohydrates, 9mg calcium, 10mg phosphorus, 0.9mg iron, 1.0mg sodium, 142mg potassium, 1,210iu vitamin A and very little vitamin B and C.

Canned purple Italian prune-type plums in water have fewer calories (46) and carbohydrates (11.9g) and more vitamin A (1,250iu) than the plums in heavy syrup.

197

POPCORN

POPPED PLAIN

100g/3½oz

Popcorn with oil and salt has 456 calories, 9.8g protein and 21.8g fat. It has 59.1g carbohydrates and 1.7g fiber. The mineral content includes a small amount of calcium (8mg) but an enormous amount of salt and sodium (1940mg) and also 216mg phosphorus and 2.1mg iron. There is some vitamin B2 (2.09mg) and 1.7mg vitamin B2.

   Sugar-coated popcorn it will have 383 calories, 85.5g carbohydrates, 6g protein and 3.5g fat. It will have very little calcium (5mg), very little phosphorus (135mg), 1.3mg iron, 1mg sodium salt and some vitamin B2 (0.06mg) and vitamin B3 (1.1mg).

   If butter is added, one must add the nutrient values of butter (see p.93) to those of plain popcorn.

NUTRITIONAL CONTENT	
Joules	1621
Calories	386
✹ Proteins	12.7g
✹ Carbohydrates	76.7g
Cholesterol	0
Fat	5g
Sat. fats	–
Unsat. fats	–
✹ Fiber	2.2g
Minerals	
✹ Phosphorus	291mg
Calcium	11mg
Iron	2.7mg
Sodium	3mg
Potassium	40mg
Magnesium	–
Vitamins	
A	0
B1	0
B2	0.12mg
✹ B3	2.2mg
B6	0.204mg
B12	–
Folic Acid	–
C	0
D	–
E	–

NUTRITIONAL CONTENT

Joules	1331.7
Calories	317
✹ Proteins	24.6g
Carbohydrates	0
✹ Cholesterol	84g
✹ Fat	23.2g
Sat. fats	–
Unsat. fats	–
Fiber	0

Minerals

✹ Phosphorus	363mg
Calcium	5.2mg
Iron	1.7mg
Sodium	66mg
✹ Potassium	308mg
Magnesium	22.6mg

Vitamins

A	trace
✹ B1	0.8mg
✹ B2	0.2mg
✹ B3	5mg
B6	0.2mg
✹ B12	1mg
✹ Folic Acid	1.5mcg
C	0
D	0
E	0.3mg

A **leg of pork** is sometimes called a leg of ham, but normally we identify a pork leg as ham only if it is salted or smoked.

This particular cut has less calories and fat, but more phosphorus and calcium than most cuts of ham.

Pork is one of the least digestible of meats. It has been proved that pork, fried ham and bacon stay longer in the stomach before being digested than other meats (chicken is the most easily digestible).

PORK: loin chops
BROILED, LEAN AND FAT
1 chop/100g/3½oz

NUTRITIONAL CONTENT	
Joules	1894
Calories	451
✳ Proteins	15.4g
Carbohydrates	0
✳ Cholesterol	84mg
✳ Fat	41.9g
Sat. fats	–
Unsat. fats	–
Fiber	0
Minerals	
Phosphorus	148mg
Calcium	6.9mg
✳ Iron	2mg
Sodium	49mg
✳ Potassium	214mg
Magnesium	12.4mg
Vitamins	
A	trace
✳ B1	0.8mg
✳ B2	0.2mg
✳ B3	5mg
B6	0.2mg
✳ B12	1.5mcg
✳ Folic Acid	1mcg
C	0
D	trace
E	0.3mg

If only the lean meat of a **grilled pork chop** is eaten, fewer calories are supplies (133), less protein (10.4g), less fat (9.7g), less sodium (31mg), less potassium (142mg), less calcium (3.8mg), less magnesium (8.5mg), less iron (1.2mg) and less phosphorus (86mg).

NUTRITIONAL CONTENT

Joules	1911
Calories	455
✱ Proteins	19.5g
Carbohydrates	0
✱ Cholesterol	84mg
✱ Fat	40.4g
Sat. fats	–
Unsat. fats	–
Fiber	0

Minerals

Phosphorus	185mg
Calcium	7.5mg
✱ Iron	2.3mg
Sodium	60mg
✱ Potassium	287mg
Magnesium	18mg

Vitamins

A	trace
✱ B1	0.8mg
✱ B2	0.2mg
✱ B3	5mg
B6	0.25mg
✱ B12	1mcg
✱ Folic Acid	1.5mcg
C	0
D	trace
E	0.3mg

If there is no fat on **roast pork loin** it contains 284 calories, 23.6g protein, half the fat of a normal roast, 69mg sodium, 353mg potassium and 23.6mg magnesium. Its vitamin content is approx. the same as that of the normal roast.

A **salted smoked loin** with only lean meat has 243 calories, 23g protein, 15.7g fat, 1800mg sodium, 300mg potassium, 27.3mg calcium, 24.1mg magnesium, 2.3mg iron and 219mg phosphorus.

PORK: spareribs

BRAISED (MED. FAT)

100g/3½oz

NUTRITIONAL CONTENT

NUTRITIONAL CONTENT

Joules	1848
Calories	440
✹ Proteins	20.8g
Carbohydrates	0
✹ Cholesterol	84mg
✹ Fat	38.9g
Sat. fats	—
Unsat. fats	—
Fiber	0

Minerals

Phosphorus	121mg
Calcium	9mg
Iron	2.6mg
Sodium	65mg
✹ Potassium	285mg
Magnesium	—

Vitamins

A	0
✹ B1	0.4mg
✹ B2	0.2mg
✹ B3	3.4mg
B6	—
B12	—
Folic Acid	—
C	0
D	—
E	—

Spare ribs with fat and **lean spare ribs** have approximately the same protein, vitamin and mineral content as **medium-fat spare ribs,** though the amount of calories and fat they contain is different.

Cooked lean spare ribs contain about 410 calories and 35g fat, while cooked fatty spare ribs contain about 467 calories and 43g fat.

Any sauce added to the ribs will, of course, increase their nutritional content.

NUTRITIONAL CONTENT

Joules	391
Calories	93
Proteins	2.6g
✸ Carbohydrates	21.2g
Cholesterol	0
Fat	0.1g
Sat. fats	—
Unsat. fats	—
✸ Fiber	0.6g

Minerals

Phosphorus	65mg
Calcium	9mg
Iron	0.7mg
Sodium	4mg
✸ Potassium	503mg
Magnesium	23.5mg

Vitamins

A	trace
B1	0.1mg
B2	0.04mg
B3	1.7mg
B6	—
B12	0
Folic Acid	0
✸ C	20mg
D	0
E	—

Potatoes baked in their skin have more nutrients than peeled boiled potatoes but less than French-fried. They retain their minerals, vitamins and energy nutrients, unlike boiled potatoes, whose nutrients are partly lost to the cooking water.

The French believe that the potato is "a perfectly digestible food, leaving no waste in the intestine." They go on to say that it has two fifths the carbohydrate of bread, is rich in potassium, and is highly desirable in diets.

Apart from its fiber content, the peel has less nutrients than the inside of the potato. To get the goodness from a baked potato, its entire content should be eaten.

Scalloped and **au gratin potatoes with cheese, butter and milk** have more calories and more vitamins than baked potatoes. They contain: 145 calories; 5.3g protein; 8g fat; 13.6g carbohydrates; 3g fiber; 127mg calcium; 122mg phosphorus; 0.5mg iron; 447mg sodium; and 306mg potassium. Their vitamin content is 320iu vitamin A, 0.06mg vitamin B1, 0.12mg vitamin B2, 0.9mg vitamin B3 and 10mg vitamin C.

Scalloped potatoes without cheese but with **milk, butter and flour** contain: 104 calories; 3g protein; 14.7g carbohydrates; 0.4mg iron; 355mg sodium; 327mg potassium; 0.09mg vitamin B2; 1mg vitamin B3; and 11mg vitamin C. They have only half the calcium of the dish made with cheese (54mg), half the phosphorus (74mg) and half the vitamin A (160iu).

POTATOES

BOILED (PEELED)
1 medium/100g/3½oz

3 small **peeled and boiled potatoes** can supply more than the minimum daily requirement of vitamin C: each potato contains 16mg of vitamin C.

The longer potatoes are stored, the less vitamin C they contain. When freshly harvested, a 3½oz (100g) potato has 26g of vitamin C; three months later, 13mg; and if stored for 6 months, only 8.6mg.

Prolonged boiling or standing before being served also causes the loss of much of the vitamin C content.

If potatoes are peeled and left standing, they will lose less vitamin C than if they are left peeled and allowed to soak uncooked in water.

A potato boiled with its skin on will retain more carbohydrates (17g), protein (2.1g), calories (76), potassium (407mg), phosphorus (53mg), slightly more vitamin B2 (0.04mg) and vitamin B3 (1.5mg).

Mashed boiled potatoes contain the same amount of nutrients as boiled peeled potatoes.

When milk is added to mashed potatoes it increases the calcium (24mg), proteins (2.1g), fats (0.7g), phosphorus (49mg), sodium (301mg), vitamin A (20iu), vitamin B2 (0.05mg) and B3 (1mg). There will be less vitamin B1 (0.08mg) and vitamin C (10mg). A portion contains 65 calories.

When fat is added to mashed potatoes with milk, the calories increase to 94, fats to 4g, sodium to 331mg and vitamin A to 170iu.

Dehydrated mashed potato flakes made with milk, water and fat have more calories (93), calcium (31mg) and fat (3.2g). They contain the same amount of protein, carbohydrates and fiber as boiled potatoes. They will contain approximately the same amount of phosphorus, potassium, iron and sodium as mashed potatoes with milk.

Dehydrated mashed potato granules made with milk, water and fat will contain similar nutrients.

The vitamin C content in dehydrated potatoes will depend on the amount contained in the potatoes before processing.

Frozen mashed potatoes when prepared contain approximately the same amount of nutrients as dehydrated mashed potatoes, but have a higher salt content (359mg).

NUTRITIONAL CONTENT	
Joules	273
Calories	65
Proteins	1.9g
✹ Carbohydrates	14.5g
Cholesterol	0
Fat	0.1g
Sat. fats	–
Unsat. fats	–
✹ Fiber	0.5g
Minerals	
Phosphorus	42mg
✹ Calcium	6mg
Iron	0.5mg
Sodium	2mg
✹ Potassium	285mg
Magnesium	–
Vitamins	
A	trace
B1	0.09mg
B2	0.03mg
✹ B3	1.2mg
B6	0.1mg
B12	0
Folic Acid	0
✹ C	16mg
D	0
E	–

NUTRITIONAL CONTENT

Joules	1151
Calories	274
Proteins	4.3g
✸ Carbohydrates	36g
Cholesterol	0
✸ Fat	13.2g
Sat. fats	3g
Unsat. fats	10g
✸ Fiber	1g

Minerals

Phosphorus	111mg
Calcium	15mg
Iron	1.3mg
Sodium	6mg
✸ Potassium	853mg
Magnesium	25mg

Vitamins

A	trace
B1	0.1mg
B2	0.08mg
✸ B3	3.1mg
B6	–
B12	–
Folic Acid	–
✸ C	21mg
D	0
E	–

Defrosted French-fried potatoes which have been heated up have less calories (220), 3.6g protein, less fat (8.4g), less carbohydrates (33.7g) and less fiber (0.7mg). They have more iron (1.8mg) but less sodium (4mg), less calcium (9mg), less phosphorus (86mg) and less potassium (652mg). There is slightly less vitamin B2 (0.02mg) and vitamin B3 present (2.6mg).

Hash-browned potatoes have 229 calories, 3.1g protein, 11.7g fat and 29g carbohydrate. They have little calcium (12mg), little phosphorus (79mg), little iron (0.9mg), 288mg sodium and 475mg potassium. They have less of the B vitamin group (0.08mg B1, 0.05mg B2, 2.1mg B3) with very little vitamin C (9mg).

Cooked defrosted hash-browned potatoes have 224 calories, 2g protein, 11.5g fat and the same amount of carbohydrate as the freshly cooked potatoes. They have 18mg calcium, more iron (1.2mg), more sodium (299mg), less potassium (283mg) and less phosphorus (50mg). The vitamin content is also lower: 0.07mg B1, 0.02mg B2, 1mg B3 and 8mg vitamin C.

Potato chips (called **crisps** in Britain) have 568 calories, 5.3g protein, 40g fat, 50g carbohydrate and 1.6g fiber. They have 40mg calcium, 139 phosphorus, 1.8mg iron, 1130mg potassium, and the vitamin content is as follows: vitamin B1, 0.21mg; vitamin B2, 0.07mg; vitamin B3, 4.8mg; vitamin C, 16mg; traces of vitamin A.

Potato sticks have approx. the same nutrients as potato chips with slightly lower calories (544), 6.4g protein, 36.4g fat and more vitamin C (40mg).

In both chips and sticks the sodium content is variable and can be as high as 1000mg per 100g.

SWEET POTATOES

BAKED IN SKIN
1 medium/100g/3½oz

The **sweet potato** with deep orange flesh contains 10000 iu of vitamin A when raw, while the light yellow fleshed type has only about 600 iu. Nevertheless there is a very high vitamin A content in all sweet potatoes, whether cooked or raw. In addition, fresh cooked sweet potato contains a goodly amount of calcium and vitamin C.

When buying sweet potatoes, buy only enough for your immediate needs as they spoil quickly.

If sweet potatoes are boiled, they lose some of their nutrients to the cooking water, but still retain about 7900 iu of vitamin A, 17mg of vitamin C and 32mg of calcium. They also have 114 calories, 1.7g protein, 0.4g fat, 26.3g carbohydrate and 0.7g fiber. The mineral content is 243mg potassium, 47mg phosphorus, 10mg sodium and 0.7mg iron.

If it is **candied,** sweet potato gains in calories (168) and in carbohydrates (34g). It has little protein, fat or fiber and loses phosphorus (29mg), calcium (13mg) and iron (0.9mg). There is more sodium (48mg) and 120mg potassium. The vitamin content is: vitamin A, 6300 iu; vitamin B1, 0.06mg; vitamin B2, 0.03mg; vitamin B3, 0.6mg; and vitamin C, 8mg.

Canned sweet potatoes in syrup still have a large vitamin A content (5000 iu), but have 114 calories, 1g protein, 27.5g carbohydrate, 6g fiber, almost no fat and less mineral content. The mineral values are: phosphorus, 29mg; calcium, 13mg; iron, 0.7mg; sodium, 48mg; potassium, 120mg.

All canned sweet potato has very little vitamin B: 0.03mg of vitamin B1, 0.03mg of vitamin B2, and 0.6mg of vitamin B3.

Canned diet sweet potatoes have reduced caloric values (46), less carbohydrate (10.8g) and less sodium (12mg), but their vitamin and mineral content is as low as that of normal canned sweet potato. The vitamin A content is 5000 iu.

Vacuum-packed sweet potatoes have an increased amount of vitamin A (7800 iu), calcium (25mg), sodium (200mg), protein (2g) and vitamin C (14mg). Their calorie content is lower (108), as is the carbohydrate content (24.9g).

NUTRITIONAL CONTENT	
Joules	592
Calories	141
Proteins	2.1g
✹ Carbohydrates	32.5g
Cholesterol	0
Fat	0.5g
Sat. fats	–
Unsat. fats	–
✹ Fiber	0.9g
Minerals	
Phosphorus	58mg
Calcium	40mg
Iron	0.9mg
Sodium	12mg
✹ Potassium	300mg
Magnesium	–
Vitamins	
✹ A	8100 iu
B1	0.09mg
B2	0.07mg
B3	0.7mg
B6	–
B12	–
Folic Acid	–
✹ C	22mg
D	–
E	–

NUTRITIONAL CONTENT

Joules	1638
Calories	390
✴Proteins	9.8g
✴Carbohydrates	75.9g
Cholesterol	0
Fat	4.5g
Sat. fats	–
Unsat. fats	–
✴Fiber	0.3g

Minerals

Phosphorus	131mg
Calcium	22mg
Iron	1.5mg
✴Sodium	1680mg
Potassium	130mg
Magnesium	–

Vitamins

A	0
B1	0.02mg
B2	0.03mg
B3	0.7mg
B6	–
B12	–
Folic Acid	–
C	0
D	–
E	–

The salt content in pretzels can vary enormously, so that very thin pretzel sticks may contain about twice the amount shown in the table.

PRUNES

DRIED, "SOFTENIZED", UNCOOKED

100g/3½oz

When **prunes** are cooked without added sugar they lose one half of their total nutrients.

When sugar is added to the cooking water the prunes retain approx. two thirds of their original energy nutrients. They will have 172 calories and 45g carbohydrates, but less minerals and vitamins than the prunes cooked without sugar (600 iu of vitamin A, 0.03mg vitamin B1, 0.06mg vitamin B2, 0.6mg vitamin B3).

Dehydrated prunes cooked with added sugar have approx. the same nutrients as softened prunes with sugar.

About one third of a cup of **prune juice** contains 77 calories, 19g carbohydrate, 4.1mg iron and a small amount of the other minerals, protein, vitamins and fat. It has no vitamin A.

Prune whip has 156 calories, 4.4g protein, 36.9g carbohydrate, 22mg calcium, 1.3mg iron, 164mg sodium, 290mg potassium and very little phosphorus. It has less vitamins than the other prune dishes, the values being 460 iu vitamin A, 0.02mg vitamin B1, 14mg vitamin B2, 0.5mg vitamin B3 and 2mg vitamin C.

NUTRITIONAL CONTENT	
Joules	1071
Calories	255
Proteins	2.1g
✱ Carbohydrates	67.4g
Cholesterol	0
Fat	0.6g
Sat. fats	–
Unsat. fats	–
✱ Fiber	1.6g
Minerals	
Phosphorus	79mg
Calcium	51mg
✱ Iron	3.9mg
Sodium	8mg
✱ Potassium	694mg
Magnesium	40mg
Vitamins	
✱ A	1600 iu
B1	0.09mg
B2	0.17mg
B3	1.6mg
B6	0.24mg
B12	0
Folic Acid	4.8mcg
C	3mg
D	0
E	–

NUTRITIONAL CONTENT

Joules	622
Calories	148
Proteins	3.1g
✷Carbohydrates	25.7g
Cholesterol	0
Fat	4.7g
Sat. fats	3g
Unsat. fats	1g +
Fiber	0.2g

Minerals

Phosphorus	96mg
Calcium	98mg
Iron	0.5mg
Sodium	56mg
Potassium	171mg
Magnesium	–

Vitamins

A	150 iu
B1	0.02mg
B2	0.14mg
B3	0.1mg
B6	–
B12	–
✷Folic Acid	–
C	trace
D	–
E	–

Vanilla pudding, made of milk, vanilla and flour, has 111 calories, the same amount of protein, fiber and phosphorus as chocolate pudding, 3.9g fat, 15.9g carbohydrate, 117mg calcium, 65mg sodium and a little potassium (138mg). It has approx. the same vitamin content.

PUMPKIN

CANNED, COOKED

100g/3½oz

NUTRITIONAL CONTENT	
Joules	139
Calories	33
Proteins	1g
Carbohydrates	7.9g
Cholesterol	0
Fat	0.3g
Sat. fats	—
Unsat. fats	—
✸ Fiber	1.3g
Minerals	
Phosphorus	26mg
Calcium	25mg
Iron	0.4mg
Sodium	2mg
✸ Potassium	240mg
Magnesium	—
Vitamins	
✸ A	6400 iu
B1	0.03mg
B2	0.05mg
B3	0.6mg
B6	0.056mg
B12	0
Folic Acid	—
C	5mg
D	—
E	—

Pumpkin is a form of squash. It may have been introduced into the American continent from Asia in times of prehistory.

Canned pumpkin is sometimes a mixture of pumpkin and winter squash.

Raw pumpkin is like canned pumpkin, but has less vitamin A (1,600iu).

Dried pumpkin seeds have large amounts of calories (553), protein (29g), fat (46.7g), carbohydrates (15g) and fiber (1.9g), as well as a large amount of phosphorus (1,144mg).

210

NUTRITIONAL CONTENT

Joules	386.4
Calories	92
✴ Proteins	13.6g
Carbohydrates	0
Cholesterol	–
Fat	3.9g
Sat. fats	–
Unsat. fats	–
Fiber	0

Minerals

Phosphorus	102mg
Calcium	5.8mg
Iron	1mg
Sodium	16mg
Potassium	107mg
Magnesium	11mg

Vitamins

A	trace
B1	0.03mg
B2	0
✴ B3	12mg
B6	0.44mg
B12	–
Folic Acid	–
C	0
D	0
E	0.7-1.1mg

Wild rabbits, frequently considered as game, are slightly tougher and have a strong flavor.

Domestically reared rabbits are tenderest at 3 months. Both are cooked the same way, and have similar nutritional content.

RADISHES
RAW
100g/3½oz

NUTRITIONAL CONTENT

Joules	63
Calories	15
Proteins	1g
Carbohydrates	2.8g
Cholesterol	0
Fat	trace
Sat. fats	–
Unsat. fats	–
Fiber	0.7g

Minerals

Phosphorus	27.1mg
Calcium	43.7mg
Iron	1.88mg
Sodium	59mg
✹ Potassium	240mg
Magnesium	11.4mg

Vitamins

A	trace
B1	0.04mg
B2	0.02mg
B3	0.2mg
B6	0.1mg
B12	0
✹ Folic Acid	10mcg
✹ C	25mg
D	0
E	0

Among the great variety of **radishes** that exist are the common, the round, the long, the pink, the black, the white, the purple, and the oriental.

They are all eaten raw. Only the **pink radish** is sometimes cooked. The leaves of the pink radish can also be eaten.

The **oriental radish** is similar to the common radish nutritionally but has less potassium.

NUTRITIONAL CONTENT

Joules	1214
Calories	289
Proteins	2.5g
✴ Carbohydrates	77.4g
Cholesterol	0
Fat	0.2mg
Sat. fats	—
Unsat. fats	—
✴ Fiber	0.9mg

Minerals

Phosphorus	101mg
Calcium	62mg
Iron	3.5mg
Sodium	27mg
✴ Potassium	763mg
Magnesium	35mg

Vitamins

A	20mg
B1	0.11mg
B2	0.08mg
B3	0.5mg
B6	0.194mg
B12	0
✴ Folic Acid	10.6mcg
C	1mg
D	0
E	—

When **raisins** are cooked with sugar and water, the dessert will have less of the energy nutrients, less minerals and very few vitamins. The energy nutrients are 56g carbohydrates, 1.2g protein and 0.1g fat, which together provide 213 calories. There will be very little calcium (29mg) or phosphorus (47mg), little iron (1.6mg), a small amount of sodium (13mg) and potassium (355mg). There will be only 10 iu of vitamin A and 0.04mg of vitamin B1, 0.03mg of vitamin B2 and 0.2mg of vitamin B3.

RHUBARB

COOKED WITH SUGAR
100g/3½oz

NUTRITIONAL CONTENT	
Joules	592.2
Calories	141
Proteins	0.5g
✸Carbohydrates	36g
Cholesterol	0
Fat	0.1g
Sat. fats	–
Unsat. fats	–
✸Fiber	0.6g
Minerals	
Phosphorus	15mg
Calcium	78mg
Iron	0.6mg
Sodium	2mg
✸Potassium	203mg
Magnesium	–
Vitamins	
A	80 iu
B1	0.02mg
B2	0.05mg
B3	0.3mg
B6	–
B12	–
Folic Acid	–
C	6mg
D	–
E	–

Defrosted sweetened rhubarb cooked with added sugar has more calories (143), more carbohydrates (36.2g), and less mineral content—especially of calcium (78mg) and potassium (176mg), and slightly less vitamin A (70 iu).

Rhubarb contains oxalic acid, which unites with the calcium making an insoluble indigestible compound. If there is any of the acid which has not been bonded, it may combine with the calcium in other foods eaten at the same time. If there is still an excess (which is unlikely) it may withdraw some of the calcium stored in the body.

RICE: ALL TYPES
UNENRICHED, COOKED
100g/3½oz

NUTRITIONAL CONTENT

Joules	457.8
Calories	109
Proteins	2g
✷ Carbohydrates	24.2g
Cholesterol	0
Fat	0.1g
Sat. fats	–
Unsat. fats	–
Fiber	0.1g

Minerals

Phosphorus	28mg
Calcium	10mg
Iron	0.2mg
✷ Sodium	374mg
Potassium	28mg
Magnesium	–

Vitamins

A	0
B1	0.02mg
B2	0.01mg
B3	0.4mg
B6	–
B12	–
Folic Acid	–
C	0
D	–
E	–

Enriched white rice when cooked contains increased iron (0.9mg) and vitamin B: B1 0.11mg; B2 0.01mg; B3 1mg; B6 0.17mg. There may be some vitamin E as well (0.6mg).

Instant cooked white rice has the same calories, fat, protein and carbohydrate content as all other rice. It has less mineral content (3mg calcium, 19mg phosphorus, a trace of potassium and 273mg sodium), but more iron than unenriched rice (0.8mg). The B vitamins are enriched as well: B1 0.13mg, B2 0.01mg, B3 1mg, B6 1.03mg.

Brown rice when cooked has slightly more of the energy nutrients, a touch more fiber, less minerals and less vitamin B1 than cooked enriched rice, though it has more minerals and vitamins than unenriched rice. It has 25.5g carbohydrate, 0.3g fiber, 2.5g protein, 0.6g fat, and supplies 119 calories. Its mineral content is 12mg calcium, 73mg phosphorus, 0.5mg iron, 282mg sodium and 70mg potassium. It contains no vitamin A but has 0.09mg vitamin B1, 0.02mg B2, 1.4mg B3, 0.55mg B6, 20.9 mcg folic acid and 2.4mg vitamin E.

Spanish rice (rice, onions, green pepper, canned tomatoes) has less carbohydrates and calories but more fat than plain rice. It has a similar mineral content but with more potassium. It gains a reasonable amount of vitamin A and vitamin C from its vegetables. It provides 87 calories and contains 1.8g protein, 16.6g carbohydrate and 1.7g fat. It contains 660 iu vitamin A and 15mg vitamin C. Its sodium drops to 216mg and its potassium rises to 231mg.

Rice pudding (rice, milk, raisins and sugar) will have more carbohydrates, three times the protein and fat, and will provide more calories. The milk will raise its calcium and iron content, but its sodium and potassium content will drop. It will gain some vitamin A as well. It has 146 calories, 3.6g protein, 3.1g fat, 26.7g carbohydrates and 0.1g fiber. Its calcium rises to 98mg, phosphorus to 94mg, and it will have 0.4mg iron. Its sodium content drops to 71mg and potassium to 177mg. There are 110 iu vitamin A, 0.14mg vitamin B2 and a trace of vitamin C.

If **polished rice** has been parboiled and dried before the bran germ (silverskin) is removed, a large amount of B1 is absorbed by the starchy part of the rice. Prepared in this way it can help to prevent beriberi.

SALAD DRESSING

MAYONNAISE
2 tablespoons/28.5g/1oz

Two tablespoons of commercially made **blue cheese or Roquefort cheese dressing** has less carbohydrate and fat but more calcium and sodium. It contains 144 calories, 1.3g protein, 15g fat, 2.1g carbohydrates, 23mg calcium, 21mg phosphorus, 313mg sodium, 10.5mg potassium, and only 0.005mg iron. The vitamin content is 60 iu vitamin A, 0.002mg vitamin B1, 0.02mg B2, 0.02mg B3, and 0.5mg vitamin C.

Low-fat blue cheese or Roquefort dressing for diets (one calorie per teaspoon) has a smaller amount of the energy nutrients but much more sodium (324mg per oz). It contains 3 calories, 0.4g protein, 0.4g fat, 0.4g carbohydrates, 10mg calcium, 7mg phosphorus, 324mg sodium, 8mg potassium, 23iu vitamin A and traces of vitamins C and B.

An ounce of French dressing has 117 calories, almost no protein (0.2g), 11g fat, 5g carbohydrate, 3mg calcium, 4mg phosphorus, a large amount of sodium (391mg), 23mg potassium and no known vitamins.

Diet French dressing (one calorie per teaspoon) still has a large amount of sodium (224mg) and the same amount of the other minerals, but less calories (3). It has 0.1g protein, 0.06g fat and 0.5g carbohydrates.

An ounce of French dressing made according to a home recipe has 180 calories, almost no protein, 20g fat, 1g carbohydrate, practically no calcium (2mg) or phosphorus (0.9mg), almost no iron (0.02mg), very little potassium (7mg) and a great deal of sodium (188mg).

Thousand island dressing contains a large amount of fat, salt and calories. In one ounce it contains 143 calories, 14g fat, 4g carbohydrate, very little calcium or phosphorus, 200mg sodium, 32mg potassium, and 91iu vitamin A, though very little vitamin B or C.

Diet thousand island dressing has the same mineral and vitamin content but will have 51 calories, 4g fat and 5g carbohydrate.

One ounce of **Russian dressing** contains 141 calories, 0.4g protein, 15g fat, 3g carbohydrate, 5mg calcium, 11mg phosphorus, 0.1mg iron, 248mg sodium and 45mg potassium. Its vitamin content is 197iu vitamin A, 0.01mg vitamin B1, 0.01mg B2, 0.2mg B3 and 2mg vitamin C.

NUTRITIONAL CONTENT

Joules	862
Calories	205
Proteins	0.3g
Carbohydrates	0.6g
Cholesterol	–
✳ Fat	23g
Sat. fats	–
Unsat. fats	–
Fiber	trace

Minerals
Phosphorus	8mg
Calcium	5mg
Iron	0.1mg
Sodium	171mg
Potassium	10mg
Magnesium	–

Vitamins
A	80 iu
B1	0.005mg
B2	0.01mg
B3	trace
B6	–
B12	–
Folic Acid	–
C	–
D	–
E	–

NUTRITIONAL CONTENT

Joules	0
Calories	0
Proteins	0
Carbohydrates	0
Cholesterol	0
Fat	0
Sat. fats	–
Unsat. fats	–
Fiber	0

Minerals

Phosphorus	trace
Calcium	253mg
Iron	0.1mg
✳Sodium	38758mg
Potassium	4mg
Magnesium	119mg

Vitamins

A	0
B1	0
B2	0
B3	0
B6	0
B12	0
Folic Acid	0
C	0
D	0
E	0

Salt is found in the sea or in the ground. Sea salt may come from the ocean or from inland brine springs. The salt water is collected and then heated until the moisture has evaporated. The higher the temperature the whiter and finer is the resulting salt. Salt from the ground is mined from underground seams of rock salt and requires purification.

The taste of sea salt is stronger than that of rock salt.

Salt is used for both flavoring and preserving, and was considered such a precious commodity in earlier times that at banquets a huge pot containing salt was placed on the table. The guests sitting at the head of the table above the salt were the honored guests, while to sit below the salt was a sign of lowliness.

SAUCES

WHITE

2 tablespoons/28.5g/1oz

This white sauce was made with milk, flour, margarine, salt and pepper.

A **sweet white sauce** would use the above ingredients minus the salt and pepper and with the addition of sugar, which provides an extra 112 calories and 30g of carbohydrate. A sweet white sauce has 153 calories and 32.8g of carbohydrate. Since sugar has almost no minerals or vitamins the other values remain unchanged.

Onion sauce will contain the nutrients of a regular white sauce with those of the amount of onion added (see *Onion*, p.00).

Tartar sauce made with mayonnaise, capers, pickle, hard-boiled egg, onion and spices contains in two tablespoonsful: 152 calories; 0.4g protein; 16.5g fat; 1.3g carbohydrate; and 0.09g fiber. Its mineral content is 5mg calcium, 9mg phosphorus, 0.2mg iron, 202mg sodium and 22mg potassium. Besides traces of the B and C vitamins, it has 63 iu of vitamin A.

Diet tartar sauce has roughly half the calories (64), very little protein, half the fat (6.4g), but more carbohydrates (1.9g). All the other nutrients are the same.

Brown sauce made with dripping, onion, turnip, carrots, bacon, flour, brown stock, herbs and spices contains in two tablespoonsful: 33 calories, 2.5g of carbohydrates, 2.2g of fat and very little protein. It has less calcium (5.7mg) and more iron (0.2mg), but otherwise the mineral content is similar to that of the normal white sauce.

NUTRITIONAL CONTENT	
Joules	172
Calories	41
Proteins	1.1g
✳ Carbohydrates	2.8g
Cholesterol	–
✳ Fat	2.8g
Sat. fats	–
Unsat. fats	–
Fiber	0
Minerals	
Phosphorus	0.01mg
Calcium	32.2mg
Iron	0.04mg
Sodium	148mg
Potassium	46mg
Magnesium	4.2mg
Vitamins	
A	800iu
B1	0.06mg
B2	0.16mg
B3	0.12mg
B6	0.04mg
B12	–
Folic Acid	0.3mcg
C	1.5mg
D	76iu
E	–

SAUERKRAUT

CANNED

100g/3½oz

NUTRITIONAL CONTENT

Joules	75.6
Calories	18
Proteins	1g
Carbohydrates	4g
Cholesterol	0
Fat	0.2g
Sat. fats	–
Unsat. fats	–
✳ Fiber	0.7g

Minerals

Phosphorus	18mg
Calcium	36mg
Iron	0.5mg
✳ Sodium	474mg
Potassium	140mg
Magnesium	–

Vitamins

A	50iu
B1	0.03mg
B2	0.04mg
B3	0.2mg
B6	0.13mg
B12	0
Folic Acid	–
✳ C	14mg
D	–
E	–

Sauerkraut juice has less calories (10), half the carbohydrates (2.4g), more iron and more sodium salt (787mg). It has little or no potassium or vitamin A. The other nutrient values are similar to those of sauerkraut.

219

SAUSAGE: Bologna

ALL MEAT

1 slice (approx. 4" diameter)

NUTRITIONAL CONTENT	
Joules	265
Calories	63
Proteins	3g
Carbohydrates	0.8g
Cholesterol	–
✸ Fat	5.2g
Sat. fats	–
Unsat. fats	–
Fiber	0
Minerals	
Phosphorus	32mg
Calcium	2mg
Iron	0.5mg
✸ Sodium	325mg
Potassium	58mg
Magnesium	–
Vitamins	
A	0
B1	0.04mg
B2	0.06mg
B3	0.7mg
B6	0.02mg
B12	–
Folic Acid	–
C	0
D	–
E	–

Bologna sausage, originally from the Italian city of Bologna, can contain cereal, in which case it will have less fat and calories and provide slightly more protein.

Mortadella, another Italian sausage, has less fat (3.5g), approx. the same amount of protein, less carbohydrate (0.1g) and less calories (45) per slice.

Liverwurst is a soft sausage which contains approx. the same amount of nutrients per slice as Bologna, but it does have a large amount of vitamin A (1350 iu per slice) and more iron (1.1mg).

Smoked liverwurst has one quarter again as many nutrients as regular liverwurst, but will be saltier. It also has a very large amount of iron and of vitamins A and B. In one ounce it contains: 90 calories, 7.8g fat, 4.2g protein and 0.7g carbohydrate. It has 1850 iu of vitamin A, 0.05mg vitamin B1, 0.41mg vitamin B2, 2.3mg vitamin B3, and 1.7mg iron.

NUTRITIONAL CONTENT

Joules	563
Calories	134
✸ Proteins	5.9g
Carbohydrates	1.1g
✸ Cholesterol	148mg
✸ Fat	11.6g
Sat. fats	–
Unsat. fats	–
Fiber	0

Minerals

Phosphorus	60mg
Calcium	3.2mg
Iron	0.06mg
✸ Sodium	499mg
✸ Potassium	99.8mg
Magnesium	–

Vitamins

A	0
B1	0.07mg
B2	0.09mg
B3	1.2mg
B6	–
B12	–
Folic Acid	–
C	0
D	–
E	–

Frankfurters can be stuffed with many ingredients. Primarily they are stuffed with beef, or pork, or with beef and pork, with non-fat dry milk and a cooked meat, with cereal and a cooked meat, or with a combination of all these and a variety of spices.

A **frankfurter** stuffed with meat and non-fat dry milk will have approx. the same nutrients as an all-meat sausage. If stuffed with cereal and meat it will have slightly fewer nutrients (less caloreis, less fat and less carbohydrates).

Bockwurst, a German pork and cereal-filled sausage which is boiled like a frankfurter but is slightly milder in taste, has marginally less nutrients, minerals and vitamins. It has 120 calories, 5g protein, 11g fat and almost no carbohydrate.

Knackwurst, shorter and fatter than the others, weighs almost twice as much and so has almost double the nutrients in each sausage. It is a mild boiling sausage, containing approx. 252 calories, 12.8g protein, 21g fat, 2g carbohydrate, 8mg calcium, 139mg phosphorus, 1.9mg iron and some vitamin B.

Sausages were created as a convenience food to use up scraps. These three popular ones have become part of the German food tradition.

SAUSAGE: salami

COOKED

1 slice (approx. 2½" diameter)

NUTRITIONAL CONTENT	
Joules	172
Calories	41
✸ Proteins	2.3g
Carbohydrates	0.2g
Cholesterol	—
✸ Fat	5.8g
Sat. fats	—
Unsat. fats	—
Fiber	0
Minerals	
Phosphorus	10mg
Calcium	1mg
Iron	0.3mg
Sodium	—
Potassium	—
Magnesium	—
Vitamins	
A	0
B1	0.02mg
B2	0.02mg
B3	0.4mg
B6	0.01mg
B12	0.0001mg
Folic Acid	0
C	0
D	0
E	—

Salami is a form of sausage: meat, fat, cereal and spices which are enclosed in a casing and then cooked. It is usually made from pork and pork products. Kosher salamis are made from beef, beef fat, cereals and spices.

Many countries have their own favorite type of national salami; there are French, German, Italian, Hungarian and Danish salamis, to name just a few.

Their exact nutritional content depends on their specific contents and, of course, will differ accordingly.

A slice will usually contain roughly the same amount of nutrients as those listed in the table.

Dried salami has more concentrated nutrients and half the water content. It contains 450 calories, 24g protein, 38g fat, 1g carbohydrate, 14mg calcium, 283mg phosphorus, 3.6mg iron and some B vitamins: 0.4mg B1; 0.3mg B2; 5mg B3.

NUTRITIONAL CONTENT

Joules	470.4
Calories	112
✺ Proteins	23.2g
Carbohydrates	0
✺ Cholesterol	52g
Fat	1.4g
Sat. fats	0.05g
Unsat. fats	0.8g
Fiber	0

Minerals

✺ Phosphorus	338mg
✺ Calcium	115mg
✺ Iron	3mg
✺ Sodium	265mg
✺ Potassium	476mg
Magnesium	–

Vitamins

A	–
B1	–
B2	–
B3	–
B6	–
B12	–
Folic Acid	–
C	–
D	–
E	–

Scallops have more protein and potassium than oysters, to which they are similar.

Scallops swim and leap about by snapping their shells. This movement is controlled by their powerful addictor muscle, the only part of the scallop we eat.

They are frequently called Coquilles St. Jacques. This name arose because of the habits of the pilgrims who visited the shrine of St. James of Campostela. Those who attended the shrine and confessed their sins were made to do penance by eating scallops. In order to show the world they had done so, they fastened the empty scallop shells to their hats.

The term *scalloped* has now come to mean any sea food which is creamed, heated and served in the shell.

There are two types of scallops, bay and sea. The small bay scallops have a more delicate taste.

When serving scallops, allow ⅓ pound for sea scallops and ¼ pound for bay scallops per person.

SEAWEED

RAW

28.5g/1oz

NUTRITIONAL CONTENT	
Joules	0
Calories	0
Proteins	0
Carbohydrates	0
Cholesterol	0
Fat	0.01–0.9g
Sat. fats	–
Unsat. fats	–
✹ Fiber	0.2–1.9g
Minerals	
Phosphorus	6–76mg
✹ Calcium	84–312mg
Iron	1.7mg
✹ Sodium	596–859mg
✹ Potassium	812–2303mg
Magnesium	–
Vitamins	
A	–
B1	–
B2	–
B3	–
B6	–
B12	–
Folic Acid	–
C	–
D	–
E	–

There are many types of seaweed and there is a large variation in the quantity of minerals they contain.

Kelp has the most calcium (312mg) and sodium (859mg) with 1507mg potassium.

Dulse has the most potassium (2302mg) with 596mg sodium and 84mg calcium.

The other seaweeds studied were **Irish moss, agar** and **laver.**

Though the vitamin content of these plants is high, care should be taken since some people (the author to name but one) have an allergic reaction to seaweed.

NUTRITIONAL CONTENT

Joules	436.8
Calories	104
✹ Proteins	21.2g
Carbohydrates	0
✹ Cholesterol	96g
Fat	1.8g
Sat. fats	–
Unsat. fats	–
Fiber	–

Minerals
✹ Phosphorus	349mg
✹ Calcium	145mg
Iron	1.1mg
✹ Sodium	1590mg
✹ Potassium	260mg
Magnesium	42mg

Vitamins
A	trace
B1	0.03mg
B2	0.03mg
✹ B3	3mg
B6	0.1mg
B12	–
✹ Folic Acid	2mcg
C	trace
D	trace
E	–

Shrimps are cooked in a salt solution.

Canned shrimps have the same values as boiled shrimps.

French-fried shrimps (dipped in egg, bread crumbs and batter and then fried in vegetable oil) have 225 calories, 20.3g protein, 10.8g fat and 10g carbohydrates.

Shrimp paste has 180 calories, 20.8g protein, 9.4g fat, 1.2g carbohydrates, no minerals and only 0.26mg vitamin B2.

SPINACH
BOILED AND DRAINED
100g/3½oz

NUTRITIONAL CONTENT	
Joules	97
Calories	23
Proteins	3g
Carbohydrates	3.6g
Cholesterol	0
Fat	0.3g
Sat. fats	—
Unsat. fats	—
✱Fiber	0.6g

Minerals

Phosphorus	38mg
Calcium	93mg
Iron	2.2mg
Sodium	50mg
✱Potassium	324mg
Magnesium	—

Vitamins

✱A	8100iu
B1	0.07mg
B2	0.14mg
B3	0.5mg
B6	—
B12	—
Folic Acid	—
✱C	28mg
D	—
E	—

Raw spinach in salad will have almost the same energy nutrients and vitamin A but will have more iron (3.1mg), potassium (470mg), vitamin C (51mg) and B vitamins: vitamin B1, 0.1mg; vitamin B2, 0.2mg; and vitamin B3, 0.6mg.

Drained canned spinach has more calcium (118mg), more salt (236mg) and less vitamin C (14mg).

Drained canned diet spinach has a reduced sodium content of 34mg.

Defrosted cooked leaf spinach has approx. the same nutrients as fresh cooked leaf spinach.

Defrosted cooked chopped leaf spinach has slightly less vitamin C (19mg) and 7,900iu of vitamin A.

Spinach contains a viscous substance which has laxative properties.

The calcium and iron in spinach cannot be used by our bodies since they are combined with other chemicals, becoming insoluble and indigestible. These chemicals, oxalic and phytic acid, may combine with iron and calcium in other foods eaten at the same time or the same meal. If there is any that has not been bonded it may well draw on the calcium and iron stored in the body. It would seem that the elderly and pregnant should not eat spinach.

NUTRITIONAL CONTENT

Joules	59
Calories	14
Proteins	0.9g
Carbohydrates	3.1g
Cholesterol	0
Fat	0.1g
Sat. fats	–
Unsat. fats	–
✹Fiber	0.6g

Minerals

Phosphorus	25mg
Calcium	25mg
Iron	0.4mg
Sodium	1mg
Potassium	141mg
Magnesium	–

Vitamins

A	390iu
B1	0.05mg
B2	0.08mg
B3	0.8mg
B6	–
B12	–
Folic Acid	–
✹C	10mg
D	–
E	–

The summer squashes are **crookneck, straightneck, white scallop, pale green scallop, green zucchini** and **cocozelle.** They all have the same nutrients, with slight variations in the vitamin A content and the amount of calories and carbohydrates.

Zucchini and **cocozelle** squash have the lowest amount of calories (12) and carbohydrates (2.5g), and contain 300iu of vitamin A when cooked. Keep the skin on them since this holds all the vitamin A.

Scallop squash have 16 calories, 3.8g carbohydrates and 180iu vitamin A when cooked.

Defrosted, boiled and drained yellow crookneck summer squash have more calories, carbohydrates, iron and potassium. They have less vitamins however. They contain 21 calories, 4.7g carbohydrate, 14mg calcium, 32mg phosphorus, 0.7mg iron, 0.3mg sodium, 167mg potassium and 140iu vitamin A. The vitamin B content is: B1, 0.06mg; B2, 0.04mg; B3, 0.4mg. They have 8mg vitamin C. (Fresh crookbacked summer squash have nutrient values similar to those shown on the main table.)

SQUASH: winter

BOILED AND MASHED

100g/3½oz

Winter squash are **acorn, butternut** and **hubbard.**

Acorn squash when boiled has the least vitamin A content (1100iu).

Butternut has 5400iu of vitamin A when boiled.

Hubbard has 4100iu of vitamin A when boiled.

All the other nutrients are approximately similar.

When the first two are baked they retain more of their nutrients. They have approx. 63 calories, 1.8g protein, 0.4g fat, 1.8g fiber and 15.4g carbohydrate. They will have slightly more calcium, phosphorus and iron than when boiled and the potassium content increases to 461mg. There are increased amounts of vitamin B: vitamin B1, 0.05mg; vitamin B2, 0.13mg; vitamin B3, 0.7mg; and the vitamin C content is approx. 13mg.

As for vitamin A content, acorn squash has 1400iu butternut has 6400iu and hubbard has 4800iu.

Defrosted winter squash when heated up has the same nutrients as fresh boiled winter squash.

228

NUTRITIONAL CONTENT	
Joules	160
Calories	38
Proteins	1.1g
Carbohydrates	9.2g
Cholesterol	0
Fat	0.3g
Sat. fats	—
Unsat. fats	—
✴Fiber	1.4g
Minerals	
Phosphorus	32mg
Calcium	20mg
Iron	0.5mg
Sodium	1mg
✴Potassium	258mg
Magnesium	—
Vitamins	
✴A	3500iu
B1	0.04mg
B2	0.1mg
B3	0.4mg
B6	—
B12	—
Folic Acid	—
C	8mg
D	—
E	—

SUCCOTASH (Corn and Lima Beans)
DEFROSTED, BOILED AND DRAINED
100g/3½oz

NUTRITIONAL CONTENT	
Joules	391g
Calories	93
Proteins	4.2g
✸Carbohydrates	20.5g
Cholesterol	0
Fat	0.4g
Sat. fats	–
Unsat. fats	–
✸Fiber	0.9g
Minerals	
Phosphorus	85mg
Calcium	13mg
Iron	1mg
Sodium	38mg
✸Potassium	246mg
Magnesium	–
Vitamins	
A	300iu
B1	0.09mg
B2	0.05mg
B3	1.3mg
B6	0.181mg
B12	0
Folic Acid	–
C	6mg
D	0
E	–

Succotash is a dish that originated with the American Indians and was adopted by the early settlers to help them weather the cold New England winters. The Indians grew sweet corn and beans together in the same plot and oftern cooked the two vegetables together. In winter, they used dried corn and beans instead of the fresh vegetables.

Succotash has a large protein, carbohydrate and potassium content. It combines two "incomplete" vegetable proteins which provide a "complete" protein when digested (see "Protein," p.22).

SUGAR (BEET or CANE)

GRANULATED

1 tablespoon/14.3g/½oz

NUTRITIONAL CONTENT	
Joules	235.2
Calories	56
Proteins	trace
✲ Carbohydrates	15g
Cholesterol	0
Fat	0
Sat. fats	–
Unsat. fats	–
Fiber	0
Minerals	
Phosphorus	trace
Calcium	0.2mg
Iron	0.005mg
Sodium	0.05mg
Potassium	0.5mg
Magnesium	0.05mg
Vitamins	
A	0
B1	0
B2	0
B3	0
B6	0
B12	0
Folic Acid	0
C	0
D	0
E	0

Sugar comes from the juice of beets or sugar cane, which is strained, refined and purified to eliminate foreign matter. During this process of purification, most of the minerals and almost all the vitamins are lost. Brown sugar and demerara sugar are the first products of the process while further refinement is necessary to produce pure white granulated sugar.

Castor sugar is granulated sugar ground fine.

Powdered sugar (icing sugar) is granulated sugar ground very fine until it has almost no discernible particles.

Brown sugar (demerara sugar) has the same calories and carbohydrates as white sugar. It has almost no vitamins. It does have a small mineral content. One tablespoonful contains 12mg calcium, 3mg phosphorus, 0.05mg iron, 4mg sodium and 49mg potassium. It contains a minimal amount of vitamin B: vitamin B1, 0.001mg; vitamin B2, 0.004mg; vitamin B3, 0.03mg.

Brown sugar also contains trace elements like chrome, cobalt, zinc and copper. Some authorities believe that the trace elements refined out of white sugar are needed by the body, and that we should therefore use less refined sugar, preferring those brown sugars "sticky from molasses."

Maple sugar made from the purified sap of sugar maple trees has 50 calories, 13g carbohydrate, 20mg calcium, 2mg phosphorus, 0.2mg iron, 2mg sodium and 35mg potassium.

NUTRITIONAL CONTENT

Joules	1344
Calories	320
✸Proteins	26g
Carbohydrates	0
✸Cholesterol	250mg
✸Fat	23.2g
Sat. fats	–
Unsat. fats	–
Fiber	0

Minerals

✸Phosphorus	364mg
Calcium	–
Iron	–
Sodium	116mg
✸Potassium	433mg
Magnesium	–

Vitamins

A	–
B1	–
B2	–
B3	–
B6	–
B12	–
Folic Acid	–
C	–
D	–
E	–

Braised calf sweetbreads provide plenty of protein, no carbohydrate and lots of cholesterol.

They contain 168 calories, 33g protein, 3.2g fat and 462mg cholesterol. They also have some vitamin B: vitamin B1; 0.06mg; vitamin B2, 0.16mg; vitamin B3, 2.9mg.

Braised lamb sweetbreads contain a fair amount of protein and a little carbohydrate.

They have 175 calories, 28.1g protein, 6.1g carbohydrate and 204mg phosphorus.

These sweetbreads are the thymus gland which is found at the top of the breast of the animal. The gland has two parts, one round and the other elongated in shape. The flesh is white and soft and also contains albumen and gelatine.

Occasionally the pancreas of a pig is sold under the name of sweetbreads.

SYRUPS

MAPLE
1 tablespoon

NUTRITIONAL CONTENT	
Joules	186
Calories	53
Proteins	0
✴ Carbohydrates	13.6g
Cholesterol	0
Fat	0
Sat. fats	–
Unsat. fats	–
Fiber	0

Minerals

Phosphorus	1.7mg
Calcium	22mg
Iron	0.2mg
Sodium	2mg
Potassium	37mg
Magnesium	–

Vitamins

A	0
B1	–
B2	–
B3	–
B6	–
B12	–
Folic Acid	–
C	0
D	0
E	–

Cane Syrup has approx. the same amount of calories and carbohydrates as maple syrup. It has less calcium and more potassium. There is also a slight amount of vitamin B present.

One tablespoonful contains: 0.13mg calcium; 89mg potassium; 0.03mg vitamin B1; 0.01mg vitamin B2; and a trace only of vitamin B3.

Sogham syrup, though similar to the other syrups in its carbohydrate and calorie content, has more calcium (3.6mg) and more iron (2.6mg).

There are more calories, carbohydrates and sodium in **blended corn syrup**, but less iron and calcium. One tablespoonful contains 61 calories, 15.7g carbohydrate, 10mg calcium, 0.9mg iron and 14mg sodium.

Blended maple and corn syrup has approx. the same calorie and carbohydrate content as the other syrups, very few minerals and no vitamins.

One tablespoonful contains traces of iron and sodium, 5mg potassium, 3mg calcium, 13.6g carbohydrates and 53 calories.

Golden syrup has more carbohydrates, which supply more calories (59). It has 16g carbohydrate, 48mg of potassium, 54 sodium and traces of iron.

NUTRITIONAL CONTENT

Joules	193.2
Calories	46
Proteins	0.8g
✳ Carbohydrates	11.6g
Cholesterol	0
Fat	0.2g
Sat. fats	—
Unsat. fats	—
✳ Fiber	0.5g

Minerals

Phosphorus	18mg
Calcium	49mg
Iron	0.4mg
Sodium	2mg
Potassium	126mg
Magnesium	7.8mg

Vitamins

A	420iu
B1	0.06mg
B2	0.02mg
B3	0.1mg
B6	0.067mg
B12	0
✳ Folic Acid	7.4mcg
✳ C	31mg
D	0
E	—

Fresh tangerine juice is similar to the whole fresh fruit in its nutrients. It does have less minerals however, and can have one or two less calories or carbohydrates depending on the quality of the fruit. It has 18mg calcium, 14mg phosphorus, 0.2mg iron, 1mg sodium and slightly more potassium than the whole fruit.

Canned unsweetened tangerine juice is nutritionally identical to fresh tangerine juice with less vitamin C (22mg).

Defrosted unsweetened tangerine juice diluted with three parts of water is also like fresh tangerine juice with 27mg vitamin C.

Sweetened canned tangerine juice has slightly more calories (50), and carbohydrates (12g). In all other respects it is similar to unsweetened canned juice.

TEA

BREWED INDIAN

1 small breakfast cup/100g/3½oz

NUTRITIONAL CONTENT	
Joules	4.2
Calories	1
Proteins	0.1g
Carbohydrates	0
Cholesterol	0
Fat	0
Sat. fats	0
Unsat. fats	0
Fiber	–
Minerals	
Phosphorus	1mg
Calcium	0.3mg
Iron	trace
Sodium	0.4mg
Potassium	17mg
Magnesium	1.1mg
Vitamins	
A	0
B1	0
B2	0.9mg
✹B3	6mg
B6	–
B12	–
Folic Acid	–
C	0
D	0
E	0

Instant tea has 2 calories, a very small amount of carbohydrates (0.4mg) and 25mg potassium per 100g. There are a number of trace elements (fiber, calcium, iron, fat and vitamin B6).

Tea contains caffeine, fluorine and tannic acid. It is bad for ulcers. Very strong tea can cause sleeplessness, palpitations of the heart and oversecretion of the gastric juices.

NUTRITIONAL CONTENT

Joules	92.4
Calories	22
Proteins	1.1g
Carbohydrates	4.7g
Cholesterol	0
Fat	0.2g
Sat. fats	–
Unsat. fats	–
✳ Fiber	0.5g

Minerals
Phosphorus	27mg
Calcium	13mg
Iron	0.5mg
Sodium	3mg
✳ Potassium	244mg
Magnesium	–

Vitamins
✳ A	900mg
B1	0.06mg
B2	0.04mg
B3	0.7mg
B6	0.1mg
B12	0
✳ Folic Acid	6.4mcg
✳ C	23mg
D	0
E	0.04mg

Summer tomatoes have more vitamin C than winter tomatoes: a medium-sized summer tomato contains 22-26mg, while its winter equivalent has 10mg.

Green unripe tomatoes have slightly more calories, carbohydrates and vitamin A than ripe tomatoes. The values are 24 calories, 5.1g carbohydrates and 270iu vitamin A.

Boiled tomatoes are nutritionally similar to ripe tomatoes, but have a slightly higher vitamin A content (1,000 iu).

Canned tomatoes are similar to ripe tomatoes but have less calcium (6mg), more sodium (130mg) and less potassium (217mg).

Canned dietary tomatoes are exactly like normal canned tomatoes, but have a very low sodium content (3mg).

Canned or bottled tomato juice is nutritionally similar to canned tomatoes, but has less fiber (0.2g), less vitamin A (800 iu) and slightly fewer calories (19).

Dietary tomato juice is normal tomato juice with less sodium (2mg).

Tomato concentrate made with 3 parts water is similar to canned tomato juice, but has 900 iu of vitamin A.

Tomato juice cocktail is similar to regular tomato juice, but has a slightly higher calorie content (21) and 5g carbohydrate.

Tomato purée has more calories, carbohydrates, sodium and vitamins than ripe tomatoes. It contains 39 calories, 1.7g protein, 8.9g carbohydrate, 1.7mg iron, 399mg sodium, 426mg potassium, 1600 iu vitamin A, 33mg vitamin C, 0.09mg vitamin B1, 0.05mg vitamin B2 and 1.4mg vitamin B3.

Tomato paste has twice the amounts of nutrients found in tomato purée.

One tablespoon of **tomato catsup** has 15 calories, 0.5g protein, almost no fat, 4g carbohydrate, 3mg calcium, 7mg phosphorus, 149mg sodium, 51mg potassium and traces of iron. It has a reasonable vitamin content: 200iu vitamin A, 2mg vitamin C, 0.02mg vitamin B1, 0.01mg vitamin B2, and 0.2mg vitamin B3.

Tomato chilli has similar nutrients.

TONGUE

PICKLED AND BOILED

100g/3½oz

NUTRITIONAL CONTENT	
Joules	1298
Calories	309
✹Proteins	19.1g
Carbohydrates	2.3
Cholesterol	–
✹Fat	23.9g
Sat. fats	–
Unsat. fats	–
Fiber	0

Minerals

✹Phosphorus	229mg
Calcium	30.9mg
Iron	3mg
✹Sodium	1870mg
Potassium	152mg
Magnesium	16.2mg

Vitamins

A	trace
B1	0.04mg
B2	0.35mg
B3	–
B6	–
B12	–
Folic Acid	–
C	0
D	trace
E	–

Braised beef tongue has 244 calories, 21g protein, 16g fat, 0.4g carbohydrate, with only 0.7mg calcium, 61mg sodium and 2.2mg iron. It has 117mg phosphorus and 164mg potassium. The vitamin B content is 0.05mg B1, 0.2mg B2 and 3.6mg B3.

Braised **hog tongue** and braised **lamb tongue** have similar nutritional values and both are within the calorie range of braised beef tongue – hog tongue has 253 calories while lamb tongue has 254.

Braised **calf tongue** has 160 calories, 23.9g protein, 6g fat and 1g carbohydrate. Thus it is higher in protein and lower in fat, carbohydrate and calories than the other types.

NUTRITIONAL CONTENT

Joules	31.9
Calories	223
✹ Proteins	31.9g
Carbohydrates	0
✹ Cholesterol	86mg
✹ Fat	9.6g
Sat. fats	–
Unsat. fats	–
Fiber	0

Minerals

✹ Phosphorus	320mg
Calcium	38.3mg
✹ Iron	3.8mg
Sodium	130mg
✹ Potassium	367mg
Magnesium	28.2mg

Vitamins

A	trace
B1	0.07mg
B2	0.16mg
B3	8.1mg
B6	–
B12	–
Folic Acid	–
C	0
D	trace
E	–

The white meat of **roast turkey** has 176 calories, 32.9g protein, 3.9g fat and 11mg of vitamin B3.

The dark meat has more vitamin B2 and more calories (203). It has 30g protein, 8.3g fat and 0.2mg vitamin B2.

Canned turkey meat has 202 calories, 20.9g protein and 12.5g fat.

Turkey pot-pie has 238 calories, 10.4g protein, 13.5g fat and 18.5g carbohydrates. It has 27mg calcium, 101mg phosphorus, 1.4mg iron, 273mg sodium and 198mg potassium. The vitamin content is high, especially in vitamin A from the vegetables: 1330 iu of vitamin A; 0.11mg vitamin B1; 0.13mg vitamin B2; 2.5mg vitamin B3; and 2mg vitamin C.

TURNIPS
BOILED and DRAINED
100g/3½oz

If you can eat **boiled turnip greens,** they will provide you with a very large amount of vitamin A, vitamin C and calcium. They also have slightly more protein and less carbohydrates than the turnips themselves. This applies to frozen or canned turnip greens as well, though they have less vitamin C. Cooked fresh turnip greens have 20 calories, 2.2g protein, 0.2g fat, 3.3g carbohydrates, and 0.7g fiber. They have 184mg calcium, 37mg phosphorus, 1mg iron, 6300 iu vitamin A, 0.15mg vitamin B1, 0.24mg vitamin B2, 0.6mg vitamin B3 and 69mg vitamin C. One 100g serving contains more than enough for the minimum daily requirement of vitamin A and vitamin C.

Canned turnip greens have 100mg calcium, 19mg vitamin C and 4700 iu vitamin A.

Cooked defrosted turnip greens have 118mg calcium, 19mg vitamin C and 6900 iu vitamin A.

Rutabagas are yellow turnips grown mostly in northern Europe. Other wise called **swedes,** they contain more carbohydrate, calories, calcium and vitamin A than normal turnips.

Cooked boiled swedes have 36 calories, 0.9g protein, 0.1g fat, 8.2g carbohydrate and 1.1g fiber. They have 59mg calcium, 31mg phosphorus, 0.3mg iron, 4mg sodium, 167mg potassium, 550 iu vitamin A, 0.06mg vitamin B1, 0.06mg B2, 0.8mg B3 and 26mg vitamin C.

NUTRITIONAL CONTENT	
Joules	97
Calories	23
Proteins	0.8g
Carbohydrates	4.9g
Cholesterol	0
Fat	0.2g
Sat. fats	–
Unsat. fats	–
✸ Fiber	0.9g
Minerals	
Phosphorus	24mg
Calcium	35mg
Iron	0.4mg
Sodium	34mg
Potassium	188mg
Magnesium	20mg
Vitamins	
A	trace
B1	0.04mg
B2	0.05mg
B3	0.3mg
B6	–
B12	–
Folic Acid	–
✸ C	22mg
D	–
E	–

NUTRITIONAL CONTENT

Joules	445
Calories	106
✱ Proteins	23.4g
Carbohydrates	0
Cholesterol	–
Fat	0.7g
Sat. fats	–
Unsat. fats	–
Fiber	0

Minerals

Phosphorus	–
Calcium	–
Iron	–
Sodium	–
Potassium	–
Magnesium	–

Vitamins

A	–
B1	–
B2	–
B3	–
B6	–
B12	–
Folic Acid	–
C	–
D	–
E	–

Turtle is a nutritious meat having a great deal of protein and very little fat or carbohydrate.

There are many types of turtles: among the edible species are the **green turtle** (the traditional ingredient of turtle soup), the **diamond back terrapin** and the **soft-shelled turtle**. Gourmets consider the flippers to be the choicest portion of the turtle.

Turtle eggs are also edible, and are eaten in many parts of the world, a practice that has led to a decline in the turtle population.

VEAL: ROAST

82% LEAN
100g/3½oz

NUTRITIONAL CONTENT

Joules	1130
Calories	269
✹ Proteins	27.2g
Carbohydrates	0
✹ Cholesterol	96mg
✹ Fat	16.9g
Sat. fats	–
Unsat. fats	–
Fiber	0

Minerals

✹ Phosphorus	248mg
Calcium	12mg
Iron	3.4mg
Sodium	80mg
✹ Potassium	500mg
Magnesium	20mg

Vitamins

A	trace
B1	0.13mg
B2	0.31mg
B3	7.8mg
B6	–
B12	–
Folic Acid	–
C	–
D	–
E	–

The figures in the table apply to a veal rib roast.

Other cuts can be used for roasting; for instance, loin of veal, round of veal, leg of veal or rolled shoulder roast. IF they have approx. 82 percent lean meat before and after roasting, their nutrient values will be the same as those shown in the table.

240

```
┌─────────────────────────┐
│ NUTRITIONAL CONTENT     │
│                         │
│   Joules      1638      │
│   Calories    390       │
│                         │
│ ✳ Proteins    23.2      │
│   Carbohydrates 0       │
│ ✳ Cholesterol 96        │
│ ✳ Fat         32.3      │
│     Sat. fats   –       │
│     Unsat. fats –       │
│                         │
│   Fiber       0         │
│                         │
│ Minerals                │
│   Phosphorus  117mg     │
│   Calcium     11mg      │
│   Iron        3mg       │
│   Sodium      80mg      │
│ ✳ Potassium   500mg     │
│   Magnesium   –         │
│                         │
│ Vitamins                │
│   A           trace     │
│   B1          0.05mg    │
│   B2          0.22mg    │
│ ✳ B3          4.2mg     │
│   B6          –         │
│   B12         –         │
│   Folic Acid  –         │
│   C           –         │
│   D           trace     │
│   E           –         │
└─────────────────────────┘
```

The veal in the table was cut from the flank and was very fatty.

The amount of fat, calories and protein in a stew will vary according to the fattiness of the meat used. A leaner meat has lower fat and calorie values and higher protein.

Stewed foreshank (86 percent lean) has 216 calories, 28.7g protein and 10.4g fat.

Plate meat (73 percent lean) has 303 calories when stewed. It has 26.1g protein and 21.2g fat.

Braised chuck meat (85 percent lean) has 235 calories, 27.9g protein and 12.8g fat.

The leaner meats contain slightly more phosphorus: approx. 150mg in chuck and foreshank, and 138mg in plate meat.

The three leaner meats have more iron (0.5mg extra).

The other nutrient values are similar to those shown on the table.

VEAL CHOP

BROILED (77% LEAN)

100g/3½oz

NUTRITIONAL CONTENT	
Joules	983
Calories	234
✸ Proteins	26.4g
Carbohydrates	0
✸ Cholesterol	96mg
✸ Fat	13.4mg
Sat. fats	–
Unsat. fats	–
Fiber	0
Minerals	
✸ Phosphorus	225mg
Calcium	11mg
Iron	3.2mg
Sodium	80mg
✸ Potassium	500mg
Magnesium	–
Vitamins	
A	trace
B1	0.07mg
B2	0.2mg
✸ B3	5.4mg
B6	0.4mg
✸ B12	0.00175mg
Folic Acid	–
C	0
D	–
E	–

This veal chop was cut from the loin.

Veal steaks and cutlets are sometimes taken from the loin. They have the same nutrients if they are broiled.

Veal steaks, chops and cutlets taken from the rump or from the leg (round) can be broiled. If they have 79 percent lean meat when broiled, they have less calories (216), slightly more protein (27g) and less fat (16.9g). They have roughly the same vitamin and mineral content.

VEAL CUTLET
BREADED, FRIED
100g/3½0z

NUTRITIONAL CONTENT

Joules	907
Calories	216
✸ Proteins	30.4g
Carbohydrates	4.4g
✸ Cholesterol	96mg
✸ Fat	8.1mg
Sat. fats	–
Unsat. fats	–
Fiber	0

Minerals

✸ Phosphorus	283mg
Calcium	10mg
Iron	2.6mg
Sodium	106mg
✸ Potassium	422mg
Magnesium	32.7mg

Vitamins

A	trace
B1	0.06mg
✸ B2	0.2mg
✸ B3	5mg
B6	–
B12	–
Folic Acid	–
C	–
D	trace
E	–

The cutlet is cut across the grain from the long round leg muscle. It is sometimes called a scallop of veal.

These cutlets must be tenderized and flattened. The tenderizing can be done by blanching, overnight soaking or by soaking for an hour in lemon juice. They are flattened by pounding with a wooden mallet or the flat side of a cleaver.

The cutlet dealt with in the table was dipped in beaten egg, then in bread crumbs, and fried in vegetable oil.

VINEGAR

DISTILLED

2 tablespoons/28.5g/1oz

NUTRITIONAL CONTENT	
Joules	4.2
Calories	1
Proteins	0.1g
Carbohydrates	0.2g
Cholesterol	0
Fat	0
Sat. fats	–
Unsat. fats	–
Fiber	0

Minerals
Phosphorus	9mg
Calcium	4mg
Iron	0.13mg
Sodium	6mg
Potassium	25mg
Magnesium	6mg

Vitamins
A	–
B1	–
B2	–
B3	–
B6	–
B12	–
Folic Acid	–
C	–
D	–
E	–

Vinegar is made from the fermentation of an alcoholic liquid and is a combination of acetic acid and water.

It can be found in the Bible used as a food flavoring; for instance, in the Book of Ruth (11:14): "At mealtime come thou hither, and eat of the bread and dip thy morsel in the vinegar."

Cider vinegar has slightly more calories and more sodium. It tastes of the cider it was fermented from and goes excellently with fresh tomatoes. It has 4 calories, 1.7g carbohydrate, a trace of protein, 1.7mg calcium, 2.5mg phosphorus, 0.17mg iron, 0.3mg sodium and 29mg potassium per ounce.

One doctor advises a mixture of honey and vinegar to cure arthritis; another advises vinegar for use in weight reduction to drive away the fat: neither seems to have anything to do with vinegar's nutritional qualities.

NUTRITIONAL CONTENT

Joules	1172
Calories	279
✸ Proteins	9.3g
✸ Carbohydrates	37.5g
Cholesterol	–
✸ Fat	9.8g
Sat. fats	–
Unsat. fats	–
Fiber	0.1g

Minerals

Phosphorus	173mg
✸ Calcium	113mg
Iron	1.7mg
✸ Sodium	475mg
Potassium	145mg
Magnesium	–

Vitamins

✸ A	330iu
B1	0.17mg
✸ B2	0.25mg
✸ B3	1.3mg
B6	–
B12	–
Folic Acid	–
C	trace
D	–
E	–

The **waffles** tested in the table were made with enriched flour, milk, eggs, fat, salt and sugar.

Waffles made with unenriched flour have less iron and vitamin B. They have 0.9mg iron and 0.05mg vitamin B1, 0.18mg vitamin B2 and 0.4mg vitamin B3.

Frozen waffles have less calories, protein, fat and vitamin A. They contain much more sodium. They contain 253 calories, 7.1g protein, 6.2g fat, 42g carbohydrate, 0.2g fiber and the following minerals: calcium, 122mg; phosphorus, 208mg; iron 1.8mg; sodium, 644mg; potassium, 158mg. The vitamin content is 130iu vitamin A, 0.17mg vitamin B1, 0.16mg vitamin B2, and 1.2mg B3.

Waffles made from a package mix with eggs and milk with enriched flour have similar enegy nutrients, much more mineral content (excluding iron) and fewer vitamins. They have 275 calories, 8.8g protein, 10.6g of fat, 36.2g of carbohydrate and 0.2g of fiber. Their mineral content is 239mg calcium, 343mg phosphorus, 1.3mg iron, 686mg sodium and 195mg potassium. They have 333iu of vitamin A, 0.1mg B1, 0.2mg vitamin B2, 0.9mg vitamin B3 and a trace of vitamin C.

WHEAT BRAN

CRUDE, COMMERCIALLY MILLED
2 tablespoons/28.5g/1oz

NUTRITIONAL CONTENT	
Joules	255
Calories	61
Proteins	4.5g
✹ Carbohydrates	17.6g
Cholesterol	0
Fat	1.3g
Sat. fats	–
Unsat. fats	–
✹ Fiber	2.6g
Minerals	
✹ Phosphorus	364.5mg
Calcium	34mg
✹ Iron	4.2mg
Sodium	2.6mg
✹ Potassium	320.2mg
Magnesium	–
Vitamins	
A	0
✹ B1	0.6mg
✹ B2	0.2mg
✹ B3	6mg
B6	–
B12	–
Folic Acid	–
C	–
D	–
E	0.1mg

Wheat bran is made from the outer coat of the cereal grain, which is removed during the bolting or sifting stage of commercial flour or meal production.

It has been used as feed for animals.

It is usually added to our diet for roughage.

It has less carbohydrates and calories, more protein and a slightly higher mineral content than bran with sugar and malt (see page 84).

NUTRITIONAL CONTENT

Joules	1529
Calories	364
✸ Proteins	10.5g
✸ Carbohydrates	76.1g
Cholesterol	0
Fat	1g
Sat. fats	–
Unsat. fats	–
✸ Fiber	0.3g

Minerals

Phosphorus	87mg
Calcium	16mg
✸ Iron	2.9mg
Sodium	2mg
Potassium	95mg
Magnesium	25mg

Vitamins

A	0
✸ B1	0.44mg
✸ B2	0.26mg
✸ B3	3.5mg
B6	0.06mg
B12	0
✸ Folic Acid	6.7mcg
C	0
D	–
✸ E	1.2mg

Unenriched all-purpose flour has less iron (0.8mg) and less B vitamins: B1, 0.06mg; B2, 0.05mg; B3, 0.9mg.

Enriched bread flour is almost identical in all its nutrients to all-purpose flour. It has one extra calorie (366), 1.3g extra protein (11.8g) and less carbohydrate (74.7g).

Unenriched bread flour has the same amount of iron and vitamin B as unenriched all-purpose flour.

Cake flour has less protein, fat, fiber and iron, and more carbohydrates. It has 364 calories, 7.5g protein, 0.8g fat, 79.4g carbohydrate, 0.2g fiber, 17mg calcium, 0.5mg iron and less vitamin B: B1, 0.03mg; B2, 0.03mg; B3, 0.7mg. It has the same sodium and potassium content as all-purpose flour but less phosphorus (73mg).

Gluten flour (45 percent gluten, 55 percent patent flour) has more calories, protein, fat, calcium and phosphorus. It contains 378 calories, 41.4g protein, 1.9g fat, 47.2g carbohydrate and 0.4g fiber. The vitamin content includes the same 0.2mg sodium found in all flours, 60mg potassium, 40mg calcium, 140mg phosphorus and little iron.

Enriched self-raising flour has less calories (352), less protein (9.3g), more calcium (265mg), more phosphorus (466mg) and a great deal of sodium. It also contains 74.2g carbohydrate, 1g fat, 0.4g fiber, and the same vitamin B and iron content as any enriched flour.

Over-refined flour has all its trace elements and most of its vitamins removed. Enrichment only replaces vitamin B3, iron and calcium. It has been suggested that chromium, zinc, copper and cobalt, vitamins B6, B12 and folic acid be replaced as well. All types of flour in Britain except 100 percent wholewheat flour must have added to them vitamins B1, B3, iron and calcium. Bread in Britain is similarly enriched, though it will not so state on the wrapper.

WHEAT GERM
CRUDE
2 tablespoons/28.5g/1oz

Toasted wheat germ cereal with added nutrients has more calories, carbohydrates, protein, potassium and vitamins than crude wheat germ.

One ounce contains 112 calories, 8.5g protein, 3.3g fat, 14g carbohydrate and 0.5g fiber. It also has 13.4mg calcium, 310mg potassium, 2.5mg iron, 0.5mg sodium, 31iu of vitamin A, 0.5mg vitamin B1, 0.25mg vitamin B2, 1.5mg vitamin B3 and 3mg vitamin C.

A great many claims have been made for wheat germ. It is said that "wheat germ can help create cellular tissue rejuvenation in the body and mind," that it can rid the body of infertility and that it is one of the richest sources of vitamin E. It is true that wheat germ has a high proportion of vitamin E, though it is by no means the only source of the vitamin. Its value as a wonder food must depend on whether you accept the claims made for vitamin E as a cure all.

It is undoubtedly a nutritious food, however, with a high caloric and potassium content.

Wheat germ is high in fat and will go rancid if kept too long.

NUTRITIONAL CONTENT	
Joules	436
Calories	104
✹ Proteins	7.6g
✹ Carbohydrates	13.3g
Cholesterol	0
✹ Fat	3.1g
Sat. fats	—
Unsat. fats	—
✹ Fiber	0.7g
Minerals	
✹ Phosphorus	319mg
✹ Calcium	21mg
✹ Iron	2.7mg
Sodium	0.9mg
✹ Potassium	236mg
✹ Magnesium	96mg
Vitamins	
A	0
✹ B1	0.6mg
✹ B2	0.2mg
✹ B3	1.2mg
B6	—
B12	—
Folic Acid	—
C	0
D	—
✹ E	4.5mg

NUTRITIONAL CONTENT	
Joules	340
Calories	81
✹ Proteins	11g
✹ Carbohydrates	11g
Cholesterol	0
Fat	0.3g
Sat. fats	–
Unsat. fats	–
✹ Fiber	0.5g

Minerals
✹ Phosphorus	501mg
✹ Calcium	60mg
✹ Iron	5mg
Sodium	35mg
✹ Potassium	541mg
✹ Magnesium	66mg

Vitamins
A	trace
✹ B1	4.5mg
✹ B2	1.2mg
✹ B3	11mg
✹ B6	0.7mg
B12	0
Folic Acid	–
C	trace
D	–
E	0.1mg

Yeasts are tiny single-cell plants which can change carbohydrates into alcohol and carbon dioxide. There are many types: some are used for fermenting grapes into wine; some are used for the raising agent in bread (the alcohol produced by the breakdown of the flour is baked off, while the carbon dioxide acts as the raising agent).

Yeasts are high in proteins and vitamins. Baking will destroy most of the vitamin content of the yeast.

Dried yeast tablets have been used to increase the B vitamins in the diet. Yeast is also being used to develop artificial protein.

YOGURT

PARTIALLY SKIMMED MILK

2 tablespoons/28.5g/1oz

Many yogurts have added vitamins and minerals. Most manufacturers add extra vitamin A, C and D.

Yogurt is a type of sour milk (fermented milk) which has been curdled to a custard-like consistency by bacteria which produce lactic acid.

It first became fashionable in the early 1900s when a famous Russian scientist, E. Metchnikoff, started to search for the secret of prolonging life. He discovered that the Bulgarians lived longer than other people in Europe at that time. Noticing that they ate an unusual type of food, yogurt, in addition to their normal diet, which was otherwise no different from that of other European countries, he assumed that their longevity must be due to this. He named the bacteria which produced yogurt *Lactobacillus Bulgaricus* (Bulgarian milk bacteria) and theorized that when these bacteria were present in the intestines, they attacked putrefying protein which makes us sick and neutralized its effects. This hypothesis has been adopted by many food faddists.

Modern analysis of yogurt shows that it is a nutritious milk food but has no special property to lengthen life. This view is supported by food scientists in the United States and abroad.

However the common belief in the health-giving properties of yogurt is a firm faith which scientific proof cannot shake.

Health food stores sell "live" yogurt. All yogurt, commercial or "health-food," contains live bacteria and is live yogurt. To prove it, make some "living" yogurt yourself. Mix 1 pint of warm milk, slightly sweetened, with a carton of natural unflavored yogurt. Keep it warm in a dark place for 5-6 hours. The bacteria in the commerical yogurt will multiply and ferment the additional milk, turning it all into live yogurt.

There is nothing to prove or disprove the health theory that yogurt taken as a convalescent food will be helpful in stimulating the growth of the body's own intestinal bacteria which may have been killed during treatment with antibiotics. Any digested food should stimulate the body's intestinal bacteria.

NUTRITIONAL CONTENT

Joules	60
Calories	14.3
✴ Proteins	1g
✴ Carbohydrates	1.5g
Cholesterol	0
Fat	0.5g
Sat. fats	—
Unsat. fats	—
Fiber	0

Minerals

Phosphorus	27mg
✴ Calcium	34.2mg
Iron	trace
Sodium	14.5mg
✴ Potassium	41mg
Magnesium	—

Vitamins

A	20iu
B1	0.01mg
✴ B2	0.05mg
✴ B3	0.03mg
B6	0.013mg
B12	trace
Folic Acid	—
C	0.3mg
D	—
E	—

NUTRITIONAL CONTENT

Joules	1777
Calories	423
✸ Proteins	10.7g
✸ Carbohydrates	74.3g
Cholesterol	0
✸ Fat	8.8g
Sat. fats	—
Unsat. fats	—
✸ Fiber	0.3g

Minerals

Phosphorus	69mg
Calcium	13mg
Iron	0.6mg
✸ Sodium	250mg
Potassium	150mg
Magnesium	—

Vitamins

A	40iu
B1	0.05mg
B2	0.07mg
✸ B3	0.9mg
B6	—
B12	—
Folic Acid	—
C	0
D	—
E	—

Zwieback is a type of dry toast. It is considered to be easily digestible.

Rusks are another form of dried toast.

There is a variety of types on sale, some of which are made with special ingredients for diets and some of which have a low sodium content. Others have reduced gluten or are specially sweetened for babies.

Their nutritional values depend on the addition or elimination of ingredients by the manufacturer.

BIBLIOGRAPHY

Basic Nutrition
Hollsworth, P. *Elementary Food Science.* London, 1974.
Pike, Magnus. *Nutrition.* London, 1961.
Schroeder, Henry A. *Trace Elements and Nutrition.* London, 1973.
Sinclair, Hugh M., and Hollingsworth, Dorothy F. *Hutchinson's Food and the Principles of Nutrition.* 12th edition. London, 1969.
Smith, D.B., and Walters, A.H. *Introductory Food Science.* London, 1966.

Statistical References
Consumer and Food Economic Institute. *Composition of Foods: Dairy and Egg Products.* Agricultural handbook no. 8-1. Washington, D.C., 1976.
Ebon, Martin. *The Essential Vitamin Counter.* New York, 1974.
McCance, R.A., and Widdowson, E.M. *The Composition of Food.* Third impression. London, 1973.
Ministry of Agriculture, Fisheries and Food. *Manual of Nutrition.* Third impression. London, 1975.
National Academy of Science. *Recommended Daily Dietary Allowances.* 8th edition. Washington, D.C., 1974.
Peterkin, B., Nichols, J., and Cromwell, C. *Nutrition Labelling.* U.S. Dept. of Agriculture Information Bulletin no. 382. Washington, D.C., 1975.
Watt, B.K., and Merrill, A.L. *Composition of Foods.* Agricultural Handbook no. 8-1. Washington, D.C. 1975.

General Reading

Atkins, R.C. *Dr. Atkins' Diet Revolution.* New York, 1975.

Cameron, Allan. *Food, Facts, and Fallacy.* London, 1971.

Davis, Elizabeth. *Salts, Spices and Aromatics in the Kitchen.* London, 1970.

Deutsch, Ronald M. *The New Nuts Among the Berries.* Palo Alto, California, 1977.

Eshleman, R. and Winston, M. *The American Heart Association Cookbook.* New York, 1975.

Goldbeck, Nan D. *Dieter's Companion.* New York, 1977.

Harben, Phillip. *The Grammar of Cookery.* London, 1965.

Hauser, Gaylord. *New Treasury of Secrets.* London, 1974.

Mackarness, Richard. *Eat Fat and Grow Slim.* London, 1975.

Montange, Prosper. *Larousse Gastronomique.* 11th impression. London, 1972.

Nilson, Bee. *Cooking for Special Diets.* London, 1974.

Passwater, Richard. *Super-Nutrition, Megavitamin Revolution.* New York, 1975.

Tannahill, Reay. *Food in History.* 1972.

Wade, Carlson. *Vitamin E: The Rejuvenation Vitamin.* New York, 1970.

World Atlas of Food. London, 1974.

Yudkin, John. *This Nutritional Business.* London, 1976.

_____. *This Slimming Business.* London, 1974.